Pressure Vessel Technology

(in three volumes)

Volume 3

Pergamon Titles of Related Interest

ASHWORTH
Corrosion: Industrial Problems, Treatment & Control Techniques

BODNER & LIEBOWITZ
Mechanics of Damage & Fracture

FARLEY & NICHOLS
Non-Destructive Testing (4-volume set)

INTERNATIONAL INSTITUTE OF WELDING
Electron & Laser Beam Welding
The Physics of Welding, 2nd Edition
Stress Relieving Heat Treatments of Welded Steel
    Constructions
Welding of Tubular Structures
Weld Quality: The Role of Computers

KETTUNEN *et al.*
Strength of Metals & Alloys (ICSMA 8) (3-volume set)

YAN *et al.*
Mechanical Behaviour of Materials V (2-volume set)

Pergamon Related Journals

(free sample copies gladly sent on request)

Acta Metallurgica

Chemical Engineering Science

Computers & Structures

Engineering Fracture Mechanics

Fatigue and Fracture of Engineering Materials & Structures

International Journal of Applied Engineering Education

International Journal of Engineering Science

International Journal of Mechanical Sciences

Materials Research Bulletin

Welding in the World

Pressure Vessel Technology

Proceedings of the Sixth International Conference held in
Beijing, People's Republic of China, 11–15 September 1988

Edited by

LIU CENGDIAN

Chinese Pressure Vessel Institution, Hefei, Anhui, People's Republic of China

and

ROY W. NICHOLS

Nichols Consultancies, Warrington, Cheshire, UK

Volume 3
The Robert Wylie Memorial Lecture
ICPVT 6 Invited Lectures
Supplementary Material

PERGAMON PRESS

OXFORD · NEW YORK · BEIJING · FRANKFURT
SÃO PAULO · SYDNEY · TOKYO · TORONTO

U.K.	Pergamon Press plc, Headington Hill Hall, Oxford OX3 0BW, England
U.S.A.	Pergamon Press, Inc., Maxwell House, Fairview Park, Elmsford, New York 10523, U.S.A.
PEOPLE'S REPUBLIC OF CHINA	Pergamon Press, Room 4037, Qianmen Hotel, Beijing, People's Republic of China
FEDERAL REPUBLIC OF GERMANY	Pergamon Press GmbH, Hammerweg 6, D-6242 Kronberg, Federal Republic of Germany
BRAZIL	Pergamon Editora Ltda, Rua Eça de Queiros, 346, CEP 04011, Paraiso, São Paulo, Brazil
AUSTRALIA	Pergamon Press Australia Pty Ltd., P.O. Box 544, Potts Point, N.S.W. 2011, Australia
JAPAN	Pergamon Press, 5th Floor, Matsuoka Central Building, 1-7-1 Nishishinjuku, Shinjuku-ku, Tokyo 160, Japan
CANADA	Pergamon Press Canada Ltd., Suite No. 271, 253 College Street, Toronto, Ontario, Canada M5T 1R5

First edition 1989

Library of Congress Cataloging in Publication Data
Pressure vessel technology: proceedings of the Sixth
International Conference, held in Beijing, People's
Republic of China, 11–15 September 1988/edited by Liu
Cengdian and Roy W. Nichols.—1st ed.
p.   cm.
Contents: v. 1. Design and analysis.
1. Pressure vessels—Design and construction—
Congresses.
I. Liu Cengdian. II. Nichols, Roy W.
TS283.P733 1988   681'.76041—dc19   88–19611

British Library Cataloguing in Publication Data
Pressure vessel technology.
1. Pressure vessels
I. Liu Cengdian   II. Nichols, Roy W.
681.76041
ISBN 0–08–035896–9

In order to make this volume available as economically and as rapidly as possible the authors' typescripts have been reproduced in their original forms. This method unfortunately has its typographical limitations but it is hoped that they in no way distract the reader.

Printed in Great Britain by BPCC Wheatons Ltd, Exeter

Contents

VOLUME 3

VOLUME 1

VOLUME 2

WYLIE MEMORIAL LECTURE

SOME RECENT TOPICS IN PRESSURE VESSEL TECHNOLOGY

T. KANAZAWA

President, The High Pressure Institute of Japan
Sampo Sakuma Building, 1-11 Kanda Sakuma-cho, Chiyoda-ku, Tokyo 101, Japan

Professor, Dept. of Industrial Management, Chiba Institute of Technology
2-17-1 Tsudanuma, Narashino City, Chiba 275, Japan

ABSTRACT

This paper, the third memorial lecture for Mr. Robert D. Wylie, reviews the
present practices and future trends in pressure vessel technology which have
arisen since the 5th International Conference on Pressure Vessel Technology
held in San Francisco in 1984. We have made tremendous progress in the
various fields of pressure vessel technology during the past four years.
Consequently, it is very difficult to review all the topics in this short
lecture. Major technical arears covered include some recent topics on
ferrous materials, fabrication techniques and life expectancy to assure
structural integrity.

KEYWORDS

Heavy gauge plates; low head ingot steel; new Cr-Mo steel; ring forged
steel; TMCP steel; narrow gap welding; arc welding robot; residual stress;
overlay; life expectancy.

INTRODUCTION

It is a great honour for me to give this 3rd memorial lecture for Mr. Robert
D. Wylie at this plenary session of the 6th International Conference on
Pressure Vessel Technology. Mr. Wylie had many Japanese friends and visited
Japan several times as a valuable adviser on the technology for nuclear
pressure vessels in Japan. Firstly in this lecture, I would like to mention
briefly the memories which many Japanese colleagues have of him, and then to
introduce some recent topics in ferrous materials and fabrication techniques
in pressure vessel technology. Lastly, I would like to refer very briefly
to the promising techniques for the life expectancy of pressure vessels.

International Conference on "Panel on Recurring Inspection of Nuclear Reactor Steel Pressure Vessels" organised by IAEA was held in Pilsen, Czechoslovakia, in October, 1966. This first international conference on nuclear reactor pressure vessels, proposed by Mr. R. D. Wylie and Prof. D. G. Latzko, was held just three years before the establishment of ASME Code, Sec. XI. It was attended by Prof. Y. Ando, Dr. S. Onodera and others from Japan.

In March, 1967, Mr. Wylie visited Japan and gave a very memorable lecture entitled "Influences of Fabrication on the Safety of Nuclear Pressure Vessels". His lecture presented design, fabrication and inspection techniques based on more than eighteen years experience in manufacturing nuclear pressure vessels in United States. Among other things, one of the phrases that most impressed the audience was "One can not inspect quality into a vessel; one must build quality into it". We still remember his words and his philosophy has recently been reiterated. His philosophy will never be forgotten as long as we manufacture nuclear components.

We were also deeply impressed by his persuasive statements at conferences or meetings concerning pressure vessel technology, whether in Japan, United States or Europe. When an awkward question was raised at such a conference or meeting, the chairman would always refer such a question to Mr. Wylie for an answer. On every occasion, his answer was clear-cut and decisive; it was always accompanied with "because..............". This "because...........", was to explain the technical background to his answer. Even members of the audience who did not agree with Mr. Wylie's initial answer, were finally convinced by his "because............".

Heat affected zone cracking under weld overlay cladding was first reported in 1972, and caused a great shock to nuclear industries throughout the world. Immediately upon receipt of this a report, Mr. Wylie brought together engineers from Europe, United States and Japan, who were also interested in such phenomena, so that this particular problem could be discussed and resolved on an international basis. A special task force on underclad cracking was established within the Pressure Vessel Research Committee of the Welding Research Council in order to investigate the problem; three subcommittees were also organized.

One year's extensive investigation, including experimentation, conducted by the Committee, clearly revealed the mechanism of cracking and produced effective remedies to deal with the problem; the significance of cracking was also evaluated. Furthermore, the brittleness of steel under conditions of "high heat input" and "very slow rate strain" during welding was also studied. The distribution and the actual value of residual stress due to overlay cladding were experimentally measured in Japan, and it was found that residual stress is one of the major causes of cracking.

Mr. Wylie showed remarkable leadership during these investigations and also in the successful preparation of the Committee's report. As far as I know, this kind of international collaboration had never been undertaken before. I firmly believe that its success was mainly due to Mr. Wylie's enthusiasm, his many friends throughout the world and their respect for him.

Mr. R. D. Wylie was killed in an air crash ten years ago in Ronneby, Sweden. On the occasion of the opening of the 6th International Conference on Pressure Vessel Technology, we would like to remember him and his contribution in this field and to hope for a deepening of international friendship and cooperation.

In the following paper, I would like to mention some recent topics in pressure vessel technology, especially, ferrous materials for pressure vessels, fabrication techniques and life expectancy of pressure vessels which will help the assurance of structural integrity.

Ferrous Materials

Heavy Gauge Plates

In recent years, reactor vessel size and operating temperature and pressure, have been increased in order to utilize pressure vessels more efficiently in oil refining and other applications. As a result, increasingly stringent requirements are being demanded of steels for pressure vessels.

A high level of cleanliness and internal soundness are the two basic requirements for these steel plates. Among the general properties, strength, low temperature toughness and weldability which are suitable for particular applications, are demanded. Quality deterioration in service must also be low. For example, Mn-Ni-Mo steel must be low in susceptibility to neutron irradiation embrittlement, and Cr-Mo steel must be low in susceptibility to temper embrittlement and hydrogen damage.

The current technology for improving the base metal properties of heavy gauge plates and the quality of plates produced by such technology will be introduced in the following. The technology for manufacturing high cleanliness steel and rolling technology for improving the internal soundness of heavy gauge plates are discussed as representative examples of heavy gauge plate production technology.

High cleanliness technology can remove impurities such as P, S, O_2 and H_2, which adversely affect the service performance of steel plates, to the lowest possible levels. A typical high cleanliness steel production process reported by Ohnishi and others (1985) is shown in Fig. 1 and Table 1. The process can remove P and S by hot metal pretreatment, and S, O_2 and H_2 by ladle refining, and can also make alloy additions. With the combination of production steps as illustrated in Fig. 1, it is a flexible process that can lower the content of impurity elements to such levels as to meet the quality requirements specified by customers.

The contents of Cu, As, Sn and Sb, which are difficult to lower using conventional refining methods, can be reduced to satisfactory levels by careful selection of scrap or by using of hot metal with low contents of such elements. A reduction refining process using calcium carbide (CaC_2) can also be used to remove these impurity elements (Kitamura and others, 1985).

It is commonly known that as a heavy gauge plate is rolled, the through thickness stress is not large enough at the mid-thickness of the plate for voids formed during solidification of ingots to be removed completely. This problem can be solved by high shape factor rolling (Nakao and others, 1979) and low speed heavy reduction rolling (Tagawa and others, 1976). The results of research carried out on the extinction of voids at mid-thickness of plates, by Nakao and others (1979), are shown in Figs. 2 and 3. The mid-thickness voids can be removed if the rolling shape factor is increased to 0.8 or above by increasing the roll diameter and reduction taken per pass. Among techniques of a similar nature developed to date are low speed heavy reduction rolling (Tagawa and others, 1984) and center portion heavy reduction rolling, or rolling a slab with mid-width projections (Tsuyama and others, 1985).

Mn-Ni-Mo steel for nuclear pressure vessels needs a room temperature tensile strength of 60 kgf/mm² class, excellent low temperature toughness and low susceptibility to neutron irradiation embrittlement. By carefully selecting the chemical composition to obtain satisfactory hardenability for low temperature toughness and by judicious selection of C content and N_2/Al ratio, these help to produce plates with properties superior to those of conventional plates, as shown in Fig. 4 (Saito and others, 1975; Nakao and Kikutake, 1976; Kikutake and others, 1980). The steel has low Cu and P contents of 0.02 % and 0.006 %, respectively, and is very low in neutron irradiation embrittlement.

Cr-Mo steel suffers from temper embrittlement, hydrogen embrittlement, hydrogen attack and creep embrittlement in service. If impurity elements, such as P, As, Sn and Sb, are removed to low levels by careful selection of raw materials and application of high cleanliness steel refining technology or if the Si content is controlled properly, steel with low susceptibility to temper embrittlement as shown in Fig. 5, can be produced (Nakajo and others, 1973; Kikutake and others, 1982). The Material Properties Council of United States has been carrying out work on the development of Cr-Mo steel with superior creep strength, elevated temperature strength and hydrogen attack resistance that can be used in lighter gauges and under higher operating temperature and pressure.

Low Head Ingot Steel

The intensity and the extension of voids and segregations at the mid-thickness of an ingot increase with the ingot size. It is impossible to produce heavy gauge steel plates with superior properties in soundness using only the rolling process without the forging process. Therefore, some special casting processes (for example: Nakagawa, 1978) have been developed, in order to produce heavy gauge plates. However, due to low productivity and high cost of these processes, there are still some problems in applying them to a commercial manufacturing process. Given these circumstances, the development of an economical technique to produce heavy gauge plates with high internal qualities has been strongly desired. A large ingot making technique utilizing the unidirectional solidification has been put forward in which commercial steels are rolled from low head ingot of up to 80 tons without forging (Nomine and others, 1979; Nakada and others, 1983; Takaishi and others, 1985).

In this section, the outline of the characteristics of low head ingots are given and the internal qualities of heavy gauge plates manufactured using the new process are explained.

Solidification profiles of low head ingots and conventional large ingots are shown in Fig. 6. The solidification in conventional ingots proceeds from both sides of the mold wall to the ingot center. In low head ingots, the ratio of the height to the width of the ingot should be as low as possible (H/D < 1.0, H: ingot height, D: ingot width). The board with exothermic and heat insulating layer/powder are set on the inner wall and the top surface of the ingot. Consequently, the solid/liquid interface is horizontal and the solidification proceeds from the bottom to the top of the ingot. The segregation and voids are localized only in the top layer of the low head ingots as shown in Fig. 7 (Yano and others, 1983; Yamada and others, 1984), and these areas can be easily removed by scarfing or machining before rolling.

Heavy gauge plates can be produced from low head ingots with superior properties in soundness and homogeneity. As mentioned above, the low head ingots show properties that are superior in soundness than conventional ingots and so the voids are easily removed during rolling as shown in Fig. 8 (Tagawa and others, 1980; 1984).

It has been reported that C-Mn steel, high tensile strength steel, Mn-Ni-Mo steel and Cr-Mo steel were rolled to heavy gauge plate of up to 333 mm thick from low head ingots, followed by low speed heavy reduction rolling process (Uemura and others, 1983; Tagawa and others, 1984). For example, Figs.9 and 10 show the results of the cleanliness, chemical analyses and mechanical properties in the direction of plate top and bottom, respectively, using 250 mm thick 2 1/4Cr-1Mo steel produced from a 40 ton low head ingot (Saeki and others, 1985).

High cleanliness is obtained and high uniformity in mechanical properties in the plate is also shown by the combination of the new ingot making technique and the very low content of impurities. Hot workability, anti-disbonding property and other characteristics of the plate surfaces corresponding to the final solidification side and the other side have been found to be satisfactory.

New Cr-Mo Steel

In the heavy oil refining and the coal liquefaction processes, higher service temperatures and pressures have been sought for efficient operation of the hydrogenation reactors. These demands for sever service conditions have called for R & D Programs to exploit heavy gauge pressure vessel steels with enhanced allowable design stress and higher resistance to hydrogen enviroments.

In United States, the R & D Program organized by the Material Properties Council, entitled by "API/MPC Program on Materials for Pressure Vessel Services with Hydrogen at High Temperature and Pressures", has been carried out since 1981 according to the time schedule shown in Table 2 (1987). In the Phase Ⅱ program, an enhanced 2 1/4Cr-1Mo steel with higher tensile strength produced by lowering PWHT temperature was developed and designated as ASME Code Case 1960. The Phase Ⅲ program to develop a V-modified 2 1/4Cr-1Mo steel to meet higher operating temperatures of up to 900°F is under way.

At the same time, NEDO (New Energy Development Organization) also began to develop a coal liquefaction reactor material as a part of the MITI/Sunshine Project of Japan. In the 5 year study from 1981, the best alloy composition to meet target values for coal liquefaction reactor materials was found to be a low Si-3Cr-1Mo-1/4V-Ti-B. In order to demonstrate the feasibility of the selected chemical composition for the production of heavy gauge pressure vessels, two heats of forged shells, the wall thickness of which were 400 mm and 450 mm respectively, were manufactured using commercial size ingots, weighing 80 and 250 tons respectively. Welding technologies such as heavy gauge girth welding by SAW and stainless steel overlay welding were also reported by Ishiguro and Watanabe (1984).

All of the data obtained in the R & D Program was submitted to ASTM and ASME B & PV Code Committee. The ASTM formally approved the 3Cr-1Mo-1/4V-Ti-B pressure vessel steel as designation No. A542 type C and A832. The ASME specified the design criteria of the developed steel in the ASME B & PV Code Case 1961.

Tables 3 and 4 show the specified values of chemical compositions and tensile properties of newly developed Cr-Mo pressure vessel steels. In the 1/4V-Ti-B added Cr-Mo steel, a lower Si content was chosen to suppress the occurrence of temper embrittlement during service at high temperature. The addition of 1/4 % V improved creep rupture strength due to the dispersion of fine vanadium carbide which resulted in increased allowable design stress as shown in Fig. 11. Small amounts of Ti and B were added to enhance hardenability and to obtain uniform distribution of tensile strength and impact toughness throughout the wall thickness of the reactor.

In the Code Case 1961 steel, the improved resistance to hydrogen attack, an important material property for hydrogenation reactors, was achieved through fine precipitations of stable vanadium carbide, due to research carried out by Ishiguro and others (1984, 1987) as shown in Fig. 12. The susceptibility to hydrogen embrittlement, which is another material problem in reactor shutdown, was evaluated based on the threshold stress intensity factor K_{IH} obtained using a rising load test. As shown in Fig. 13, the 3Cr-1Mo-1/4V-Ti-B steel was confirmed to have lower susceptibility to hydrogen assisted cracking compared with conventional 2 1/4Cr-1Mo steel. As a result of researches by Ishiguro (1987), the improved resistance is considered to be due to lower diffusibility of hydrogen in the Code Case 1961 steel at ambient temperature.

Ring Forged Steel

For large sized pressure vessels used in oil refineries and nuclear reactors, large forgings are sometimes used to reduce welding lines. For example, recent nuclear reactor pressure vessels have been produced using large forged shell rings. In order to produce heavy gauge , large scaled forged rings of high quality, a clean and homogeneous ingot with low impurities must be made. To do this, the ultra clean steel making techniques for heavy gauge steel plates as described above are used. As regards ingot making techniques, hollow ingot making techniques have been developed in Japan (Takeda and others, 1983; Aso and others, 1986) and in Europe (Palengat and others, 1985).

To produce large forged shell rings, hollow ingots which are initially ring shaped are used in addition to ordinary solid ingots. For example, Aso and others (1986) reported that a 320 ton hollow ingot has been used for the production of the shell ring of a 1100 MWe BWR pressure vessel which is now being built in Japan. Many researchers (Palengat and others, 1985; Aso and others, 1986) found that since the material is cooled from both inner and outer surfaces in a hollow ingot, the control of cooling can place the final solidification line in the mid-thickness and thus inverse V segregation lines are prevented from appearing on the inner surface of the final product. Therefore, the use of hollow ingots is effective in preventing under bead cracking when the inner surface of the pressure vessel is overlayed. Because of the short solidification time for a hollow ingot, the segregation of chemical composition is light. Figure 14 shows the distribution of C content over the thickness of a 250 ton hollow ingot reported by Aso and others (1986). The C content varies within ± 0.02 %, indicating that the ingot is almost homogeneous.

On the other hand, a multi-pouring (MP) method is used to make large solid ingots of up to 600 ton in order to reduce segregation. Takenouchi and

Suzuki (1987) showed the distribution of the C content in an ingot made by the MP method as shown in Fig. 15. The C distribution is more isotropic than using conventional methods.

Examples of tensile and impact properties and fracture toughness reported by Koshizuka and others (1985), and Aso and others (1986) are shown in Figs. 16 ~ 18 for Mn-Ni-Mo steel forging, produced from a 220 ton hollow ingot which was made for the shell ring of a 1300 MWe PWR pressure vessel. The difference in mechanical properties is small as regards the position in the ingot (from top, middle and bottom) and direction, indicating the isotropy of the ingot. As a whole, the mechanical properties are very good, although the strength at the mid-thickness is a little lower than that at other positions resulting from a mass effect. Fracture toughness is also so good that the material has a satisfactory margin to safety.

Koshizuka and others (1985) reported that the shell ring made from a hollow ingot as shown in Fig. 19 had such low Cu and P content that irradiation embrittlement is small. Takenouchi and Suzuki (1987) investigated the mechanical properties of a shell ring made from a solid ingot produced using the MP method for a PWR pressure vessel as shown in Fig. 20. They also reported the manufacture of SUS 304 forged shell ring of FBR pressure vessel named "Monju", whose dimensions were 7.2 m in outer diameter, 50 mm in thickness and 4 m in height. For desulfurizers in oil refinery, around 400 mm thick 2 1/4Cr-1Mo steel forged shell rings were also produced by Japanese steel makers (Aso and others, 1983; Kohno and others, 1983; Takenouchi and others, 1987).

TMCP Steel

Recentry, steel plates which have excellent weldability and high fracture toughness have been produced by thermo-mechanical control process (TMCP) and these plates are utilized in many kind of structures such as ships, offshore structures, bridges and pressure vessels etc. The manufacturing process and the characteristics of these steels are introduced in the report of the sub-committee on pressure vessel steel organized by the Japan Pressure Vessel Research Council (JPVRC) (1986). TMCP steels are basically classified into two types; non-accelerated cooling (non-AcC) process type and accelerated cooling (AcC) process type. Figure 21 shows a schematic diagram comparing TMCP with conventional rolling.

Non-AcC process consists of low slab reheating temperature and intensifi-cation of rolling reduction in the austenite unrecrystallization region. The controlled rolling is finished either in the region of austenite or in the intercritical region, i.e. austenite-ferrite ($\gamma + \alpha$). In AcC process, accelerated cooling is carried out after controlled rolling. In TMCP process, cooling rate and finish-cooling temperature are versatile, depend-ing on the required properties.

The metallurgical changes of TMCP steel during the process from slab reheating (austenite region) to final cooling (transformation process) are schematically shown in Fig. 22. Improvement in strength and toughness is mainly brought about through the ferrite grain refinement in non-AcC process and through the ferrite grain refinement and transformation strengthening in AcC process. Direct-quenching (DQ) process introduced by Watanabe (1983) can be defined as a kind of AcC process and improves the strength and toughness through the enhancement of hardenability compared with the conventional quenching process as shown in Fig. 23. Therefore, TMCP enables the reduction of the amount of alloying elements or carbon equivalent for the production of a given strength level as shown in Fig. 24.

Since TMCP steel is characterized by its low C and low carbon equivalent (Ceq), the hardenability, cold cracking susceptibility and toughness of HAZ, TMCP steel has shown improvements compared with conventional steels. Figures 25 ∼ 27 show examples of the improvements of HAZ properties.

Another characteristic of TMCP steel is high crack arrestability to brittle fracture as shown in Fig. 28. Due to the inherent characteristics of TMCP method, the plates cannot be formed at elevated temperatures without sustaining significant loss in strength as shown in Fig. 29, and consequently should be hot worked heated to a temperature not exceeding 600 ℃.

In Japan, on-line accelerated cooling apparatuses were installed in the rolling lines of plate mills in the early 1980's (Tsukada and others, 1982; Akiyama and others, 1983; Onoe and others, 1983; Shiga and others, 1983; Ohotani and others, 1984). TMCP steel have been widely applied to ship building, offshore structures, line pipes, pressure vessels etc. The total amount of TMCP steel produced in Japan reached over two million tons up to the end of 1986.

Recently, European mills have also installed on-line accelerated cooling apparatus in order to benefit from the characteristics of TMCP steel (Bufalini and others, 1984; Gräf and others, 1985; Wilmotte and others, 1985).

At present, TMCP has already been approved for the production of structural steels by major ship classification societies, JIS, ASTM and API. JIS G 3115, Steel Plates for Pressure Vessels for Intermediate Temperature Service (SPV); JIS G 3126, Carbon Steel Plates for Pressure Vessels for Low Temperature Service (SLA); ASTM A-841-86, Steel Plates for Pressure Vessel, Produced by the Thermo-Mechanical Control Process (TMCP) and ASTM A-844-86, Steel Plates, 9 % Nickel Alloy, for Pressure Vessels, Produced by the Direct-Quenching Process are the standards for steel plates for pressure vessels. API 2W, Specification for Steel Plates for Offshore Structures, Produced by Thermo-Mechanical Control Processing (TMCP) is a standard for offshore structures. Furthermore, the High Pressure Gas Safety Institute of Japan conducted a joint study on the application of TMCP steel for pressure vessels, and confirmed the good performance of TMCP steel plates in 1987.

FABRICATION

Narrow Gap Welding

With the recent increase in demand for large welded structures using heavy gauge plates, the assuarance of high quality in welded joints has become an unavoidable subject. Narrow gap welding has been extensively applied world wide to various kinds of large welded structures such as pressure vessels, boilers, buildings, bridges and offshore structures.

In Japan, the definition of narrow gap welding was discussed by the subcommittee on Weld Metal & Welding Procedures of JPVRC and formulated as "a technique to weld heavy gauge plates of more than 30 mm thickness either by a mechanical or an automatic arc welding process and preparing a narrow gap groove compared with the plate thickness (the gap is smaller than approximately 20 mm when the plate thickness is less than 200 mm and smaller than approximately 30 mm when the plate thickness is more than 200 mm)". This welding technique, enabling considerable minimization of the sectional area of the groove and efficient welding without excess heat input, has achieved cost savings and good productivity in high quality welded joints (Stalker and others, 1979; Sejima and others, 1981; Malin, 1983).

The technical commission on welding processes of the Japan Welding Society (1986) revealed that practical applications of narrow gap welding techniques mainly by the gas shielded arc welding process have been rapidly promoted as shown in Fig. 30.

Narrow gap welding is conducted by MAG, TIG and SAW welding processes. Of these processes, MAG is the most popular for narrow gap welding. Various kinds of welding methods and equipment, as shown in Table 5, have been developed in order to obtain enough penetration into the side wall of the groove. In narrow gap welding, the most important point in the welding procedure is generally to prevent lack-of-fusion into the side wall of the groove without generation of any other defects.

The advantage of this process compared with the SAW process is that preheating and interpass temperatures can be kept low, because the process uses no flux and the hydrogen content of the weld metal is low. On the other hand, this process presents a problem in maintaining the gas shielding conditions, requiring a countermeasure against wind in many cases and also requires special welding equipment.

The TIG welding process can provide high quality joints and beautiful bead appearance in all welding positions. The field of application of this process, however, has previously been rather restricted since the welding efficiency is lower than that of other welding processes. Recently, demand for higher quality joints in all welding positions has become so large that the TIG welding process has been re-evaluated and various attempts to improve TIG welding efficiency have been made both in terms of welding procedure and welding equipment as shown in Fig. 31 (Saenger and Manz, 1968; Takeuchi and Nagashima, 1986).

Examples of established narrow gap welding using the TIG welding process are as follows: a process to effectively use the magnetic field generated by a direct current charged into a filler wire for deflection of the arc in the welding direction developed by Tanaka and Hashimoto (1981) and by Takeuchi and Nagashima (1986) (MC-TIL process, Fig. 32), and a hot wire TIG process using a low frequency pulse arc current proposed by Hori and others (1986) (HST process, Fig. 33). This process is generally applied to welding of higher grade steel or in any position.

The most important factor in narrow gap welding using the SAW process is slag removability after each welding pass. Recent study of the relation between the physical properties of the generated slag in the molten state and after solidification and the detachability of the slag has made considerable progress. Welding flux with good slag removability has also been developed exclusively for narrow gap welding by many researchers (Tanaka and Hashimoto, 1981; Hirai and others, 1981; Kumagai and Okuda, 1984).

In this situation, practical application of this process has become possible. The practical advantages of this process are that the condition of arc light, fume and wind do not need to be considered, conventional standard equipment can be utilized, and the deposition rate is comparatively large.

As in any other narrow gap welding process, improper selection of welding conditions can cause pear-shaped penetration and hot cracking. In the SAW process, welding penetration is so deep that the selection of proper welding conditions is important in the prevention of hot cracking. Proper welding conditions should be set by considering not only crack resistance but also incomplete fusion, bead shape, slag removability and other factors. Figure 34 shows a typical macrosection of a welded joint.

In addition, semi-narrow gap welding using the SAW process where each layer receives two welding passes has recently been widely applied. Ducort and others (1979), and Tanaka and Hashimoto (1981) show that this process causes a small reduction in efficiency, but has great advantages in terms of slag removability and soundness of the welded joint, as well as greater flexibility in welding conditions. Sugioka and Sueda (1986) indicate three variations in the narrow gap SAW process and their features as shown in Table 6.

The application of narrow gap welding has various advantages. However, the welding process requires not only the provision of special equipment and consumables in some cases but also synthetic supports such as groove preparation, edge alignment, prevention of welding deformation and welding conditions. The general advantages and disadvantages of narrow gap welding application are shown in Table 7. In order to perform trouble-free narrow gap welding, it is necessary to understand the process and take the necessary countermeasures. Lastly, a guide to narrow gap welding in Japan has been published by the Technical Commission on Welding Processes of the Japan Welding Society (1986).

Arc Welding Robot

According to a survey by the Japan Welding Engineering Society's Committee on Robotic Arc Welding, welding robots used in boilers and pressure vessels, including robots designed exclusively for this use, there are about 70 robots at work in various products. In terms of the type: commercially available robots, commercially available partially modified robots and user developed robots account for one third each of all applications.

From the point of view of the welding process, gas shielded arc welding such as CO_2 and MAG is the most common while there are only a few applications of TIG and SAW. From the point of view of the control method, 60 % utilize teaching-playback and some 30 % numerical control. In terms of mechanism, 60 % are cartesian-coordinate type while the rest are revolute type. This greater number of cartesian-coordinate type robots is a marked feature and is due to the fact that suitable shapes and sizes of work and joint configuration are carefully chosen for the application of this type of robot.

Nakayama (1987) examines the locations where working arc robots are presently used as shown in Fig. 35. From this figure, one can see that the majority are circumferencial and longitudinal drum joints, followed by flange to drum joints, nozzle to drum and circumferencial pipe joints in this order. For comparatively long joints such as circumferential and longitudinal joints, however, cartesian-coordinate manipulator type robots used as conventional automatic welding machines seem to be in the majority. Consequently, those used exclusively for narrow gap welding as described in the previous section occupy almost all the applications.

The present state of the application of robotic welding using revolute type robots is mainly described below. When considering the application of arc welding robots to the kind of products mentioned above, the versatility of revolute type robots, which are considered to be typical arc welding robots, should be used to the fullest full extent in order to enhance the effectiveness of their application. Therefore, when selecting structural members to be welded by robots, it is effective to apply them to joints which are sufficiently numerous to allow repetition of the same welding condition and to heavy gauge members where multi-pass welding under similar welding conditions can be made.

Some examples of application to typical structures are as follows:

(1) The application to cylindrical structures.
This system was developed by Mitsubishi Heavy Industries, Ltd. and is composed of a 6-axis revolute type robot mounted on a large-sized manipulator and a turn table. It is applied to butt welding of circumferencial joints and vertical upward welding. The maximum thickness for this particular application is 50 mm (Figs. 36 and 37).

(2) Branch welding.
The application of welding robots to the foot of a branch of comparatively large diameter in relation to the main structure has also been developed by Mitsubishi Heavy Industries, Ltd. A welding robot for this aplication exclusively is used since the amount of weld at the same location is large (Fig. 38). The significant feature of this type of robotic welding is that the main procedure is one layer by one pass welding and, in many cases, numerical control is used jointly with teaching-playback as well as teaching-playback alone.

(3) Nozzle welding.
Welding of small diameter nozzles to the main structure by robot is employed by Kawasaki Heavy Industries, Ltd. and Mitsubishi Heavy Industries, Ltd. Since there are numerous nozzles and the welding working spots are distributed widely along the longitudinal axis, there are two types of application as shown in Figs. 39 and 40. One type developed by Kawasaki Heavy Industries, Ltd. is shown in Fig. 39, where the work piece is fixed and the robot moves as it welds. The other type developed by Mitsubishi Heavy Industries, Ltd. is shown in Fig. 40, where the robot is fixed and the work piece moves as welding progresses.

(4) Pipe welding.
In this application, the most common occurrence is where the pipes are fixed and the robot travels on a rail fastened to the circumference of the pipe. In Fig. 41, which shows an example used by Toshiba Corp., penetration welding from one side or the other is generally required. Thus TIG welding is mainly applied to this type of welding.

Although the practical application of welding robots to pressure vessels and boilers is not at such an advanced state as compared with automobiles or construction machinery, great efforts are being made to apply the technique to work such as nozzles and branches which require comparatively repeated welding. It should be admitted, however, that there are not a few difficulties in the practical application of robots to structures of diversified, small lot production. At the same time, the most important question from the man-hour and cost saving point of view is which route should be taken: either the use of an arc welding robot or the exclusive use of an automatic welding machine.

It must be kept in mind that the following problems must be solved before promoting practical application to these kinds of structure.
(1) Standardization and simplification of joint design.
(2) Easy handling through unification and systemization of the arc welding robot and the apparatus related to the positioner.
(3) Development of an arc welding robot which is flexible and suitable for diversified, small lot production.
(4) Development of easy to handle, compact arc welding robots with adaptive control functions.
(5) Increase in accuracy of work dimension.

Overlay

Stainless steel cladding is applied to the inside surface of pressure vessels for nuclear power and chemical plants in order to provide corrosion resistance.

In the early stages of overlay technique, metal arc welding, TIG welding and submerged arc welding (SAW) with a single wire electrode, series submurged arc welding with two wire electrodes or multi-electrode submurged arc welding were used in the fabrication of pressure vessels. In Japan, SAW process with a 75 mm wide strip electrode was studied early in the 1960's, and this technique was employed in the fabrication of boiling water reactor (BWR) vessels for suplying electric power (784 MW) from 1974. A superior method to SAW was developed early in the 1970's and was applied to overlay welding for components of actual plants such as the BWR power plant (1100 MW) from 1982. Figure 42 shows the overlay on the reactor pressure vessel mentioned above. This overlay welding is electro-slag welding (ESW) with a 150 mm wide strip electrode.

In the case of SAW, the cladding is produced with electric arc heat. In the case of ESW, on the contrary, the arc is supressed by using specially composed flux. The characteristic feature of this technique lies in the fact that the steel plates to be welded are fused not only by the heat from the electric arc, as in all other versions of arc welding, but also by means of molten flux whose temperature is much higher than the melting point of the steel. The cladding properties such as low dilution from base metal, homogeneous chemistries and low slag inclusion, therefor, result.

Large welding currents, such as 2500 A, increase the magnetic field and give rise to a serious pinch effect which results in irregular overlays with undercuts. An effective remedy for eliminating the influence of the magnetic field is the addition of an anti-magnetic field. Figure 43 illustrates schematicaly this principle. Lorentz force induced through two electro-magnet coils agitates the molten pool towards both sides of the overlay bead. This force dimnishes the undercut at the edge of the overlay bead and flattens the surface of the overlays as shown in Figs. 44 and 45.

European manufactures first found cracks in the weld heat affected zone of ASME SA508 class 2 steel after removing the cladding, and a large number of investigations have been undertaken on an international scale to determine the causes of this type of cracking (Vinkier and Pense, 1974; Kume and others, 1976). The under clad cracking occurs directly beneath the overlap area of the overlay beads as shown in Fig. 46 and propagates transversely to the welding direction along grain boundaries during postweld heat treatment. No cracks are found in the cases of low heat input welding processes. Heat input is the main contributory factor for under clad cracking.

Susceptibility to underclad cracking depends markedly on the chemistry of the base metal. The following equation may predict underclad cracking tendency;

$$\triangle G = [Cr] + 3.3 \, [Mo] + 8.1 \, [V] - 2$$

where [Cr], [Mo] and [V] are concentrations in weight percent of alloy in the elements present.

When $\triangle G$ is positive, the steel is susceptible. This equation suggests that SA 508 class 2 (0.4 % Cr - 0.6 % Mo steel) is susceptible to cracking while SA 508 class 3 (0.2 % Cr - 0.5 % Mo steel) is less susceptible. Consequently, the latter class 3 steel is currently used for BWR in Japan.

In the case of austenitic stainless steel cladding on SA 508 class 2, there exists a very high peak stress (about 400 MN/m²) just beneath the overlapped area of the strip cladding beads as shown in Fig. 47. The elastic and/or plastic strain also increases due to the differential expansion of the stainless steel cladding and the low alloy steel base metal during postweld heat treatment. The highest strain values are estimated at 0.23 % using a finite element method. The heat-affected zone of crack-susceptible SA 508 class 2 steel shows low elongation at post weld heat treatment temperature, i.e., 0.22 % at 615 °C. Such cracks are formed, as a result of the relaxation of strain exceeding the creep ductility of the coarse-grained heat-affected zone during stress relieving.

In petroleum processing vessels such as the hydro-desulfurizing reactor of a hydrocracker, the weld cladding which is made of heavy gauge plate of 2 1/4 Cr-1 Mo steel using austenitic stainless steel strip electrode has incurred hydrogen enrichment after prolonged exposure to high pressure and high temperature hydrogen gas. The resulting disbonding of the cladding is one problem of particular concern to the industry (Naitoh and others, 1980; Morishige and others, 1985). A remedy for this type of hydrogen-induced cracking is the technique of surface induction heating as shown in Fig. 48. In addition, the use of this induction heating before postweld heat treatment results in a fine-grained structure directly beneath the cladding and a greater resistance to underclad cracking (Kume and others, 1976).

As mentioned above, the overlay welding technique has been developed to give a higher melting rate with increasing welding current. In addition to the current overlay technique, various improvements in technique such as

employing soft plasma, low-vacuum plasma, laser beam or diffusion bonding
have recently been developed.   These improvements have the advantage of
avoiding underclad cracking and deterioration of base metal properties.

Residual Stress

Weld residual stress sometimes plays a very important role which can
significantly affect the structural integrity of a plant.   For example,
Inter-Granular Stress Corrosion Cracking (IGSCC) has been one of the biggest
concern for Boiling Water Reactors (BWR) during past ten years.   It has
occured at heat affected zones of girth weld of austenitic stainless steel
pipe where weld residual stress is very high and is considered as one of the
most important factors.   Many techniques to lower residual stress have been
developed and some of them have been successfully implemented in actual
plants.   In the following, some topics relating to residual stress
improvement are reviewed.   These techniques are heat sink welding (HSW)
(Kirihara and others, 1979), induction heating stress improvement (IHSI)
(Umemoto and Tanaka, 1978), backlay welding (BLW) (Brust and Rybicki, 1981),
and last pass heat sink welding (LPHSW) (Kraus, 1986).

HSW was mainly developed in Japan.   It requires cooling the inside surface
of the pipe with water during the weld after the first two or three layers.
Using this inside-cooling, a very large temperature difference is generated
between the outer and inner surfaces, and compressive residual stresses are
induced on the inner pipe surface.   Many experiments (Kirihara and others,
1979; Sasaki and others, 1980) and analyses (Shimizu and others, 1984; Ueda
and others, 1984) have been conducted to verify the validity of HSW.   A
typical example of experimental results is shown in Fig. 49.   The residual
stress of HSW for a pipe greater than 4" become compressive stress.   It was
also revealed that sufficient cooling is essential to obtain compressive
stresses.   Other analytical and experimental studies by Brust and Stonesifer
(1981), and Umemoto and others (1983) showed that a higher heat input is
required for thicker pipes and also that local repair welds should be
avoided because high tensile stress may be induced even if water cooling is
applied during the repair.

The IHSI technique was also developed in Japan.   It consists of heating the
outer pipe surface by induction coil and simultaneously cooling the inner
surface with water.   This process induces sufficient temperature difference
between the outer and inner pipe surfaces to produce plastic flow which re-
distribute the weld residual stress.   IHSI is applied after the completion
of welding and is applicable to almost all shapes of pipe including straight
pipe, reducer, elbow, branch, cap, plug weld and so on (Ishikawajima-Harima
Heavy Industries Co.,Ltd., 1981; Rybicki and McGuire, 1984).   Figure 50 is
one example of the many verification test results, showing that the tensile
residual stress changed to the compressive side through this treatment.
Umemoto and others (1980), Herrera and others (1982) , and Shadley and his
colleagues (1982) showed IHSI can suppress not only the initiation of IGSCC

but also the growth of existing cracks. It has also been revealed by the researches conducted by Hughes and others (1982), Shimizu and others (1984), and Nakamura and others (1986) that IHSI can improve fatigue life as well as suppress the growth of existing fatigue cracks as shown in Fig. 51.

In order to obtain successful results, some parameters, called essential variables, should be maintained within the specified ranges. These ranges were clearly established by Tanaka and Umemoto (1980), Umemoto and others (1983), and Rybicki and McGuire (1981; 1984). A judgement of whether IHSI has been performed correctly or not is easily made by checking these essential variables. Further advantages are that IHSI need not cut or re-weld the joint welds already installed and treatment time is comparatively short. Since very large diameter pipes are very difficult to replace, the IHSI method has mainly been applied to large pipes (Fig. 52). More than two thousand joints ranging up to 28 inches in diameter have been successfully treated in Japan and other countries since the first application in August 1977.

The BLW method consists of overlaying weld metal on the outer surface of the pipe near the joint with simultaneous cooling of the inner surface. According to research by Umemoto and his colleagues (1983), the length and thickness of backlay is very important to achieve successful results. The controlling range of these parameters depends on the welding condition of the backlay and the pipe dimensions as shown in Fig. 53. The overlay weld is considered as an additional allowance of the pipe wall and can compensate for any cross sectional area lost due to cracking. Consequently, this method is usually used when the existence of IGSCC is a concern. Unfortunately, ultra-sonic testing through the backlay is not easy (Park and others, 1987) and requires a special technique such as the inclined longitudinal wave method.

As weld residual stress is usually dominated by the last welding pass, it can be expected that the residual stress can be improved by inner surface cooling to only the last welding pass (LPHSW technique). Brust and Stonesifer (1981) showed by FEM analysis that LPHSW can produce weld residual stress compression as shown in Fig. 54. This method is also applicable to a completed joint by using a TIG torch without filler metal. LPHSW does not require additional weld metal on the outer surface and the usual non-destructive testing methods can be applied without difficulty. However, in order to obtain compressive stress, weld heat input should be increased with increases in pipe thickness (Herrera, 1984; Umemoto and Tanaka, 1986). From this view point, LPHSW is not suitable for thick pipes as extremely high heat input is required.

LIFE EXPECTANCY

Increases in electric power plants and chemical industry plants operating over very long-terms and the tendency toward severe operating conditions have led to an increased need for improved life expectancy and extention technology for these plants. For example, Fig. 55 shows estimated age distribution of electric power plants, excluding nuclear plants, in United States in every ten year commencing with 1970.

Methods for determining the degree of damage may be roughly divided into (a) the theoretical analysis method, (b) the dissectional examination and (c) the non destructive examination method. The theoretical method is effective as a means of predicting damage, although its accuracy is not sufficient at present and detailed operational records are needed. On the other hand, the dissectional examination method and the non destructive examination method show directly the damage accumulated during service.

Haneda and his colleagues (1985) show the present status of non-destructive defect inspection and quantitative damage evaluation due to fatigue and creep as shown in Table 8. A quantitative determination of defects will become indispensable, and this subject is being intensively studied around the world (Kimura, 1977; Ishii, 1978; Dover and Collins, 1980).

Information on the residual life of equipment is much sought after for facilities used under high temperature and stress over a long period, such as thermal power plants. Of the damage factors which rule the residual life of such equipment, creep damage is the most dominant factor while damage in component is composed of mechanical and metallurgical damage. Mechanical damage such as creep voids, microcracks and macrocracks, is being researched, using fracture mechanics and damage mechanics.

In addition, metallurgical study currently under way in this field refers to metallurgical damage which includes the precipitation of the sigma phase in austenitic stainless steels as well as the type and form change in carbides in low alloy steels. At present, various non destructive techniques are proposed to detect creep damage as shown in Fig. 56. However, among these many techniques, the replication method has already been applied to actual equipment in Germany (Auerkori and others, 1983), and in Japan (Haneda and others, 1985). The extraction replica method has also been thoroughly researched as the most promising technique to detect creep damage at an early stage and has been applied practically in Japan (Haneda and others, 1985).

Masuyama and others (1987) investigated the quantitative analysis of micro-structural change in 2 1/4Cr-1Mo steel weldment which had been used for pressure parts in a thermal power plant comparing it with the creep rupture data and creep-fatigue damage analysis results. Based on this much wider range from the total system point of view, Figs. 57 and 58 show the system for life extention and metallurgical assessment proposed by them.

In order to establish a more reliable assessment of life expectancy, there are many subjects which need to be studied in the future such as:
(a) Enhancement in the precision of life consumption estimation in cyclic

load conditions at high temperature and development of a crack propagation
life estimation method.
(b) Improvement in the precision of the quantitative determination of
defects by non destructive inspection.
(c) Practical development of much more reliable non-destructive defect
detecting technology.

ACKNOWLEDGEMENTS

The author is very grateful to the following colleagues in the preparation
of this draft: especially, Mr. Y. Sakai, Mr. Y. Nishikawa, Mr. Y. Fukuhara
and Mr. H. Nakano, Kobe Steel Ltd.; Mr. K. Ohtani, Mr. H. Takashima, Dr. Y.
Hagiwara and Dr. J. Kobayashi, Nippon Steel Corp. ; Mr. T. Shimoda, Nippon
Kokan K. K.; Dr. S. Onodera and Mr. S. Tomizuka, The Japan Steel Works,
Ltd.; Mr. S. Aoki and N. Nishiyama, Kawasaki Steel Corp. ; Dr. K. Bessho,
Sumitomo Metal Industries Ltd.; Mr. M. Amano, Mr. K. Okabayashi and Mr. T.
Umemoto, Ishikawajima-Harima Heavy Industries Co., Ltd.; Mr. F. Kanatani and
Mr. S. Nakayama, Kawasaki Heavy Industries, Ltd.; Dr. H. Yajima, Mitsubishi
Heavy Industries Ltd.

REFERENCES

Ferrous Materials

Akiyama, N. and others (1983). J. Iron Steel Inst. Japan, 69, S. 1267.
Aso, K. and others (1983). Kawasaki Steel Giho, 15, 249-257.
Aso, K. and others (1986). Kawasaki Steel Tech. Report, 15, 65-73.
Bufalini, P. and others (1984). Proc. Int. Conf. HSLA Steels, Wollongong,
    Australia.
Graf, M. and others (1985). Proc. Sympo. Accelerated Cooling of Steel, 165-
    180, The Ferrous Metallurgy Committee of the Metallurgical Soc. of AIME.
High Pressure Gas Safety Inst. Japan (1987). Study Report on TMCP Steel
    Plates.
Ishiguro, T. and J. Watanabe (1984). ASME Publication, MPC-21, 43-51.
Ishiguro, T. (1987). J. Iron Steel Inst. Japan, 73, 1, 34-40.
Kikutake, T. and others (1980). Proc. 4th Int. Conf. Pressure Vessel
    Technology, 1, 397-401.
Kikutake, T. and others (1982). Proc. Pressure Vessels and Piping Conf.,
    223-235.
Kitamura, K. and others (1985). J. Iron Steel Inst. Japan, 71, 220-   .
Kohno, K. and others (1983). R & D Kobe Steel Tech. Report, 33, 3, 12-24.
Koshizuka, N. and others (1985). Proc. IAEA Specialists' Meeting on "Recent
    Trends in Primary Circuit Technology, Madrid, Spain.
Materials Properties Council (1987). MPC Report, HPV-39.
Nakada, M. and others (1983). J. Iron Steel Inst. Japan, 69, 11, 67-73.
Nakagawa, Y. (1978). J. Iron Steel Inst. Japan, 64, 12, 113-129.

Nakajo, Y. and others (1973). Proc. 3rd Int. Conf. Pressure Vessel Technology, II, 1011-1017.
Nakao, H. and T. Kikutake (1976). J. Iron Steel Inst. Japan, 62, 4, S.271.
Nakao, H. and others (1979). Winter Annual Meeting of AIME, 119-135.
Nomine, M. and others (1979). J. Iron Steel Inst. Japan, 65, 11, S.697.
Ohnishi, Y. and others (1985). Iron & Steel Maker, 12, 2, 29-34.
Ohtani, H. and others (1984). J. Iron Steel Inst. Japan, 70, A209-A212.
Onoe, Y. and others (1983). Nippon Steel Tech. Report, 22, 1-17.
Palengat, R. and others (1985). Proc. 10th Int. Forging Conf., 13.1-13.9, Sheffield, England.
Report of Subcomm. on Pressure Vessel Steel (1986). Japan Pressure Vessel Research Council (JPVRC).
Saeki, T. and others (1985). J. Iron Steel Inst. Japan, 71, 4, S.267.
Saito, A. and others (1975). J. Iron Steel Inst. Japan, 61, 12, S.748.
Shiga, C. and others (1983). Proc. Int. Conf. Tech. and Appl. HSLA Steels, ASM.
Tagawa, H. and others (1976). J. Iron Steel Inst. Japan, 62, 13, 1720-1733.
Tagawa, H. and others (1980). NKK Tech. Report, 86, 265-274.
Tagawa, H. and others (1984). Proc. 5th Int. Conf. Pressure Vessel Tech., II, 864-877.
Takaishi, S. and others (1985). J. Iron Steel Inst. Japan, 71, 4, S.265.
Takeda, M. and others (1983). Kawasaki Steel Tech. Report, 7, 16-26.
Takenouchi, T. and others (1987). J. Iron Steel Inst. Japan, 73, 7, 778-785.
Tsukada, K. and others (1982). NKK Tech. Report, Overseas, 35, 24-34.
Tsuyama, S. and others (1985). J. Iron Steel Inst. Japan, 71, 6, 712-718.
Uemura, M. and others (1983). NKK Tech. Report, 100, 20-32.
Watanabe, S. and others (1983). Proc. Sympo. Appl. TMCP Steels to Welded Structures, 63-92, Soc. Nav. Arch. Japan.
Wilmotte, S. and others (1985). Proc. Sympo. Accelerated Cooling of Steel, 181-194, Ferrous Metallurgy Comm., The Metallurgical Soc. of AIME.
Yamada, M. and others (1984). Proc. 5th Int. Conf. Pressure Vessel Tech., II, 1300-1309.
Yano, K. and others (1983). NKK Tech. Report, 100, 11-19.

Fabrication

Brust, F. and R. B. Stonesifer (1981). EPRI NP-1743, EPRI.
Brust, F. and E. F. Rybicki (1981). J. Pressure Vessel Tech., 103, 3, 226-232.
Ducrot, M. and others (1979). IIW XII-B-260-79.
Fujimura, H. and others (1986). Mitsubishi Juko Giho, 23, 1, 10-12.
Herrera, M. L. and others (1982). ASME Publication 82-PVP-60, ASME.
Herrera, M. L. (1984). ASME Publication 84-PVP-38, ASME.
Hirai, Y. and others (1981). IIW XII-A-009-81.
Hori, K. and others (1986). Report Tech. Comm. Welding Process, JWS.
Huges, N. R. and others (1982). J. Pressure Vessel Tech., 10, 4, 344-350.
Ishikawajima-Harima Heavy Industries Co., Ltd. (1981). EPRI NP-81-LD, EPRI.

Kawasaki Heavy Industries Ltd. (1987). Internal Tech. Report, 1-2.
Kirihara, S. and others (1979). J. Japan Weld. Soc., 48, 10, 756-762.
Krause, G. T. (1986). Welding J., 65, 5, 21-29.
Kumagai, M. and N. Okuda (1984). Quart. J. Japan Weld. Soc., 2, 2, 10-15.
Kume, R. and others (1976). J. Engg. Mat. and Tech., 98, 348-356, ASME.
Malin, V. Y. (1983). Welding J., 62, 4, 22-30.
Mitsubishi Heavy Industries, Ltd. (1987). Welding Technique, 35, 2, 102-103
Naitoh, K. and others (1980). J. Pressure Engg., 18, 5, 271-276, HPIJ.
Nakamura, H. and others (1986). ASME Publication 86-PVP-103, ASME.
Nakayama, H. (1987). Tech. Review, 115, 19-22, Boiler and Crane Safety Ass.
Norishige, N. and others (1985). Trans. Japan Weld. Soc., 16, 1, 12-18.
Park, J. Y. and others (1987). Proc. SMiRT, D 2/4, 249-254.
Rybicki, E. F. and others (1981). ASME Publication 81-PVP-31, ASME.
Rybicki, E. F. and P. A. McGuire (1984). ASME Publication 84-PVP-37, ASME.
Saenger, J. F. and A. F. Manz (1968). Welding J., 47, 5, 386-393.
Sasaki, R. and others (1980). Proc. EPRI Seminar Countermeasures for BWR
  Pipe Cracking, EPRI.
Sejima, I. and others (1981). J. Japan Weld. Soc., 50, 11, 50-56.
Shadley, J. R. and others (1982). ASME Publication 82-PVP-45, ASME.
Shono, S. (1986). Welding Technique, 34, 5, 55-59.
Shimizu, T. and others (1984). Int. J. Pressure Vessels and Piping, 16, 3,
  299-319.
Stalker, W. L. and others (1979). Metal Construction, 4, 185-190.
Sugioka, I. and A. Sueda (1986). Report Tech. Comm. Welding Processes, 177-
  181, JWS.
Suruga, S. and others (1987). Welding Technique, 35, 9, 62-66.
Takeuchi, N. and M. Nagashima (1986). Report Tech. Comm. Weld. Processes,
  135-141, JWS.
Tanaka, S. and T. Umemoto (1980). Proc. EPRI Seminar Countermeasures BWR
  Pipe Cracking, EPRI.
Tanaka, K. and Y. Hashimoto (1981). R & D Kobe Steel Engg. Reports, 31, 4,
  77-80.
Tech. Comm. Welding Processes (1986). JWS.
Ueda, Y. and Others (1984). ASME Publication 84-PVP-10, ASME.
Umemoto, T. and S. Tanaka (1978). IHI Engineering Review, 18, 1, 29-37.
Umemoto, T. and others (1980). Proc. 4th Int. Conf. Pressure Vessel Tech.,
  1, 131-137.
Umemoto, T. and others (1983). Proc. 6th Post SMiRT Conf.
Umemoto, T. and Y. Tanaka (1986). IHI Engineering Review, 26, 4, 230-235.
Vinckier, A. G. and A. W. Pense (1974). WRC Bulletin, 197, Aug.

Life Expectancy

Dover, W. D. and R. Collins (1980). British J. NDT., 22, 6, 291-295.
Elect. Power Research Inst. (1986). CS-4778, Research Project 2596-1, Final
  Report, June.
Haneda, H. and others (1985). Tech. Review, October, 217-224, Mitsubishi
  Heavy Industries, Ltd.

Ishii, Y. (1978). J. NDI Japan, 27, 1, 2.
Kimura, K. (1977). J. NDI Japan, 26, 5, 308.
Masuyama, F. and others (1987). Proc. 3rd Int. Conf. Creep of Engineering Materials and Structures, 879-894.
Sada, T. and others (1987). Technical Report, 24, 3, 255-261, Mitsubishi Heavy Industries, Ltd.
Suto, Y. and others (1987). Proc. Sympo. Safety and Reliability of Structures, 213-218, Japan Science Council.

Table 1. Operating condition of NSR system

Steps	Outline of treatment
Pretreatment	150 t/heat KR agitation (Fluxes : CaO, CaF, Scale)
BOF	150 t/heat
VSC	Slag thickness : 20 mm Slag softener addition
IP	Flux addition rate : 100 - 200 kgf/min Carrier gas flow rate : 60 - 120 Nm/hr
LF	Fluxes : CaO, Al O , CaF, SiO Transformer capacity : 15,500 KVA
RH	Ordinary method in RH degasser

Table 2. The API/MPC five year research program
on hydrogenation reactor materials

Phase I	An evaluation and summary of the data on reactor material properties collected by API consultants in 1981-1982. During one year, beginning June, 1983.
Phase II	A study of the properties of 2 1/4Cr-1Mo steel of 85-110 ksi UTS, and collection of data to support an ASME code case. During three years, beginning June, 1983.
Phase III	A study of higher performance alloy modified Cr-Mo steels for service in H_2, to 900°F. Tentatively a two year program, starting date no earlier than 1984.

1656

Table 3. Chemical compositions for the
newly developed pressure vessel
steels specified by ASTM standard

Ele-ment	Conventional 2 1/4Cr-Mo [1]	Enhanced [2] 2 1/4Cr-1Mo	3Cr-1Mo- [3] 1/4V-Ti-B
C	0.15 max.	0.11/0.15	0.10/0.15
Mn	0.30/0.60	0.30/0.60	0.30/0.60
P	0.035 max.	0.015 max.	0.025 max.
S	0.035 max.	0.015 max.	0.025 max.
Si	0.50 max.	0.50 max.	0.10 max.
Cr	2.00/2.50	2.00/2.50	2.75/3.25
Mo	0.90/1.10	0.90/1.10	0.90/1.10
Cu	——	0.25 max.	0.25 max.
Ni	——	0.25 max.	0.25 max.
V	——	0.02 max.	0.20/0.30
Ti	——	——	0.015/0.035
B	——	——	0.001/0.003

(1) A 387 Gl.22   (2) A 542 / A 542 M Type B
(3) A 542 / A 542 M Type C, A 832 / A 82M-84

Table 4. Tensile properties for the newly developed
pressure vessel steels specified by ASTM

	Conventional 2 1/4Cr-1Mo	Enhanced 2 1/4Cr-1Mo	3Cr-1Mo-1/4V-Ti-B
TS, ksi (kgf/mm^2)	75/100 (52.8/70.4)	85/110 (59.8/77.4)	85/110 (59.8/77.4)
0.2% YS, ksi (kgf/mm^2)	45 min. (31.7 min.)	55 min. (38.7 min.)	60 min. (42.2 min.)
El. %	18 min.	20 min.	18 min.

Table 5. Flat position narrow gap GMA welding process

Welding method	1	2	3	4	5
Principles	Using wire deformed plastically into waved shape to produce oscillating arc at root face.	Using twisted electrode consisted of two interwinded wires to produce rotational movement of arc.	Using wire deformed plastically into corrugated shape to produce oscillating arc at root faces.	Rotate the wire with constant curvature to produce oscillating arc.	Using the spiral type of wires to produce rotational movement of arcs.
Wire (Diameter)	Solid (1.2)	Solid (2.0, 2.0)	Solid (1.2)	Solid (1.2)	Solid (1.2)
Shield gas	$Ar-CO_2$ (20%)	$Ar-CO_2$ (10-20%)	$Ar-CO_2$ (20%)	$Ar-CO_2$ (20%)	$Ar-CO_2$ (20%)
Power sources	DC (Pulse)	DC (Dropping)	DC (Pulse)	DC (Pulse)	DC (CP or Pulse)
Groove (Gap, Bevel angle)	I groove (9 mm)	I groove (14 mm)	V groove (1-4")	I groove (11 mm)	I groove
Polarity	DC (EP)	DC (EP)	DC (EP)	DC (EP)	DC (EP)
Current (A)	280 - 300	480 - 550	260 - 280	290 - 310	300 - 360
Voltage (V)	29 - 31	30 - 32	29 - 30	28 - 30	31 - 35
Welding speed (cm/min.)	20 - 28	20 - 37	18 - 22	20 - 27	20 - 30
Frequency of oscillation	60 - 80/min.	—	250-900/min.	20 - 60/min.	120-150/min. (Spiral dia. 2.5, 3.0 mm)
Remarks	BHK method	Twist-Arc method	Corrugated wire method	Loop Nap method	Rotational movement of arc

Table 5. Flat position narrow gap GMA welding process (Continued)

Welding method	6	7	8	9
Principles	Using rotating contact tip with an eccentric guid hole to produce rotating arc in high speed.	MIG welding with alternating current using large diameter wire.	Welding with alternating current using flux cored wire in Ar-CO_2 shielding system.	Wire oscillation with mechanical waving of contact tip in double gas shielding system.
Wire (Diameter)	Solid (1.2)	Solid (4.0, 4.8)	Flux cored wire (2.9, 3.2)	Solid (1.6)
Shield gas	Ar-CO_2 (20%)	Ar-CO_2 (5-10%)	Ar-CO_2 (20%)	CO_2
Power sources	DC (Pulse)	AC	AC	DC (CP)
Groove (Gap, Bevel angle)	I groove (16-18 mm)	I groove (13 mm)	I groove (10 mm)	I groove (13 mm)
Polarity	DC (EP)	—	—	DC (EP)
Current (A)	300	600	400	320-380
Voltage (V)	33	28	28	12-38
Welding speed (cm/min.)	25	30	30	25-35
Frequency of oscillation	max. 150 Hz	—	—	45/min.
Remarks	Rotating arc in high speed	AC-MIG	SMAC method	NOW-B method

Table 6. Variations of "SUBNUP" process and their features

Method	Groove and pass sequence	Applicable plate thickness (mm)	Features	Points to be considered
The small angular-X-groove method	(a) 30°~40° Cut Wire / (b) 30°~40° Cut Wire	~80	• Most effective in saving of welding time and materials for the plate thickness of 40 to 80 mm • Capable of no back-gouging, method (b)	• Unfused part in needs to be removed by back gouging or welding of the 1st pass of backside • Use of special flux of excellent slag removal
The single center pass method	3° 6R	~150	• Most effective in saving of welding time and materials for the plate thickness over about 70 mm	• Hot crack on 1st pass on high C steel • Fairly severe control of welding conditions • Use of special flux of excellent slag removal
The two pass layer method	2° 8R	~300	• Most applicable to over 150 mm thick plate • Easy slag removal • Wide range of allowable welding conditions • Exellent toughness by small heat input	• Use of special flux of good slag removal and good bead contour

Table 7. Advantages and disadvantages of narrow gap welding

Advantages	Disadvantages
(1) Reduction of welding time	(1) Difficulty in repair welding
(2) Reduction of the cost of welding materials	(2) Need for advanced welding skill
(3) Improvement of joint toughness	(3) Adjustment of target point of electrode
(4) Reduction of welding deformation	(4) Accuracy of groove preparation

Table 8. Non-destructive damage detecting method

Method	Damage		Detecting factors
	Fatigue	Creep	
Microstructure	—	◎	Change in kind and quantity of precipitate elements
σ-phase	—	◎	Change in σ-phase quantity
Creep void	—	◎	Change in creep void quantity
Hardness	◎	◎	Change in hardness
X-ray diffraction	◎	◎	Change in half width
Eddy current	—	◎	Change in eddy current
Electric resistivity	—	◎	Change in electric resistivity
Ultrasonic	◎	—	Changes in ultrasonic propagation properties
Magnetic	◎	—	Changes in magnetic properties

Pretreatment		B O F	N S R				Products				
TDS	KR		VSC	IP	LF	RH	Chemical composition (ppm)				
CaO + N₂	O₂ Flux	O₂	Vac	Flux+Ar	Flux	Alloy Vac					
							[P]	[S]	[H]	[O]
I	○	○	○	○	(○)	○	○	50	10	1.5	15
II	○	—	○	○	(○)	○	○	120	10	1.5	15
III	○	—	○	○	○	—	○	120	20	1.5	—
IV	○	—	○	○	—	—	○	120	50	1.5	—
V	○	—	○	(○)	—	—	○	150	50	1.5	—

Fig. 1. NSR system for producing clean steel

$$\frac{\ell}{h_m} = \frac{\sqrt{R(h_0 - h_1)}}{1/2(h_0 + h_1)}$$ (Shape factor)

$$X = \frac{B_0 - B_1}{B_0} = 1 - \frac{B_1}{B_0}$$ (Deformation ratio of void in through thickness direction.)

$$Y = \frac{A_0 - A_1}{A_0} = 1 - \frac{A_1}{A_0}$$ (Deformation ratio of void in rolling direction.)

Fig. 2. Schematic illustration of ℓ/h_m, X and Y

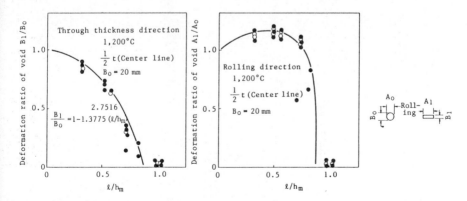

Fig. 3. Effect of shape factor on deformation ratio (B_1/B_0) and (A_1/A_0)

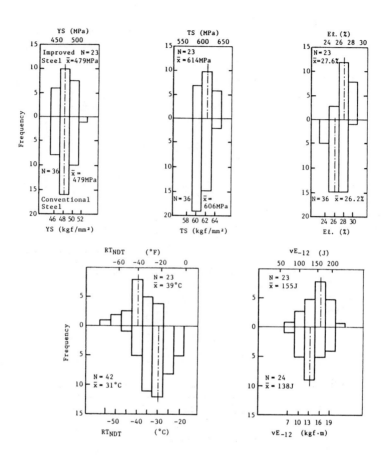

Fig. 4. Distribution of mechanical properties and fracture toughness in improved and conventional A533B Cl. 1 steel

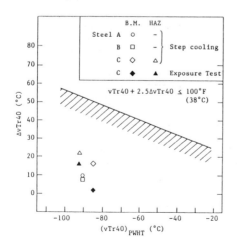

Fig. 5. Temper embrittlement of A 387-22 steel plate produced by BOP

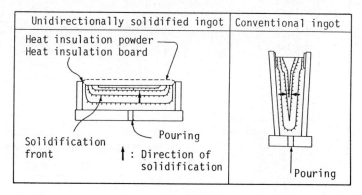

Fig. 6.　Comparison of solidification profile

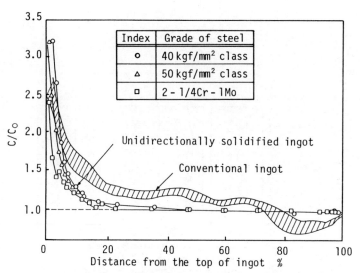

Index	Grade of steel
○	40 kgf/mm² class
△	50 kgf/mm² class
□	2 - 1/4Cr - 1Mo

Fig. 7.　Carbon segregation ratio at the center line of the
unidirectionally solidified ingot and conventional
big end top ingot

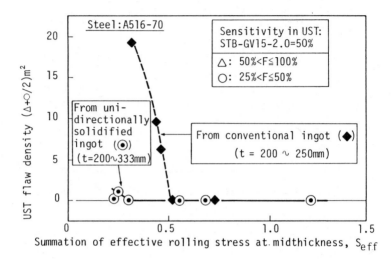

Fig. 8. Influence of S_{eff} on UST flaw density of A 516-70 steel
plates rolled from unidirectionally solidified ingots

$$\left(\begin{array}{l} S_{eff} = \Sigma(\sigma_{max}/\kappa_0 - 1), \quad \sigma_{max}/\kappa_0 \geq 1 \\ \sigma_{max} : \text{Maximum compressive stress at midthickness} \\ \kappa_0 \quad : \text{Uniaxial flow stress} \end{array}\right)$$

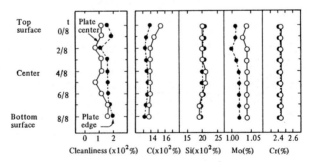

Fig. 9. Distribution of cleanliness and chemical
elements (250mm thick 2 1/4Cr-Mo steel plate)

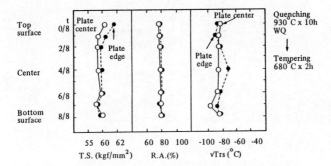

Fig. 10. Distribution of mechanical properties
(250mm-thick 2 1/4Cr-1Mo steel plate)

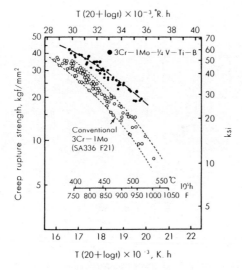

Fig. 11. Creep rupture strength of
the 3Cr-1Mo-1/4V-Ti-B
pressure vessel steels
compared with conventional
3Cr-1Mo steels

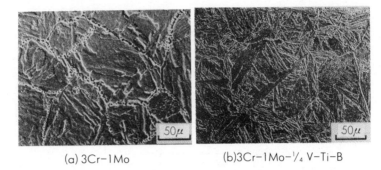

(a) 3Cr–1Mo   (b)3Cr–1Mo–¼ V–Ti–B

Fig. 12. Comparison of hydrogen attack resistances between
conventional 3Cr-1Mo HAZ and 3Cr-1Mo-1/4V-Ti-B HAZ
exposed to 650°C/30Mpa hydrogen

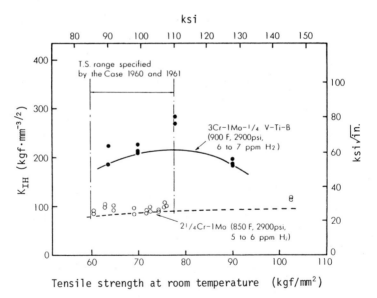

Fig. 13. Tensile strength versus K_{IH} of 2 1/4Cr-1Mo and
3Cr-1Mo-1/4V-Ti-B steels

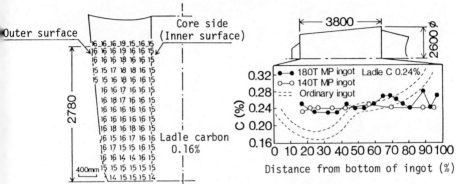

Fig. 14. Distribution of carbon in
a 250 ton hollow ingot

Fig. 15. Distribution of carbon in core
area of solid ingot by multi
pouring

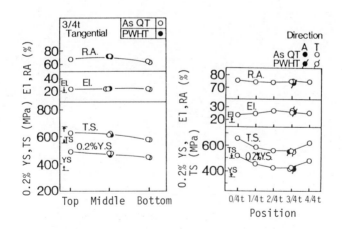

Fig. 16. Tensile properties at room temperature
shell ring
(Forged from 220 ton hollow ingot)

1668

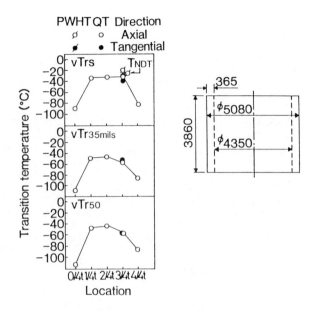

Fig. 17. Charpy impact test results over the wall thickness of a shell ring (Forged from 220 ton hollow ingot)

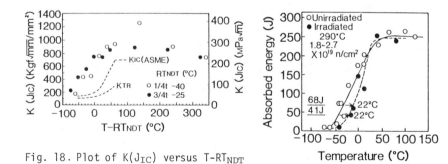

Fig. 18. Plot of K(J_{IC}) versus T-RT$_{NDT}$

Fig. 19. Effect of neutron irradiation on the Charpy absorbed energy transition curve of a shell ring forged from 200 ton hollow ingot

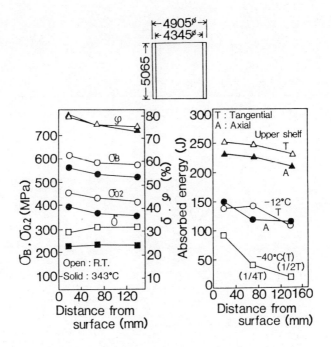

Fig. 20. Tensile and impact properties through thickness
of a shell ring forged from solid ingot

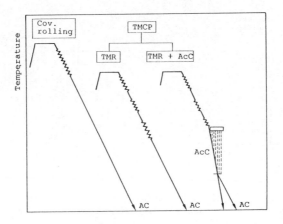

Fig. 21. Schematic illustration of
thermo-mechanical control
process
[TMR:Thermo-mechanical rolling]
AcC:Accelerated cooling
[AC :Air cooling   ]

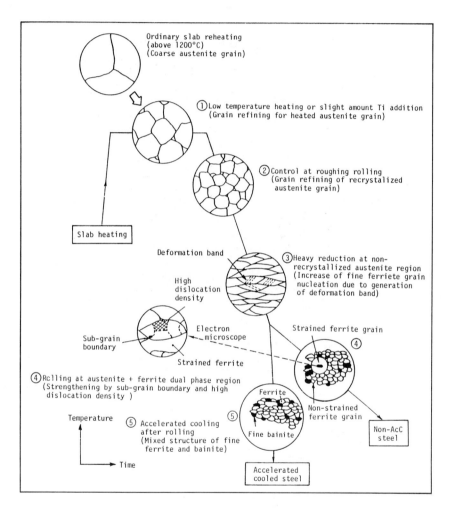

Fig. 22. Microstructural changes of austenite and subsequent transformation during TMCP

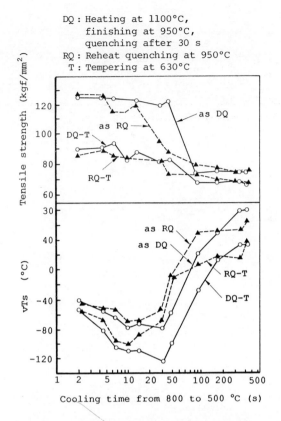

DQ : Heating at 1100°C,
     finishing at 950°C,
     quenching after 30 s
RQ : Reheat quenching at 950°C
 T : Tempering at 630°C

Fig. 23. Influence of cooling speed
         at quenching upon strength
         and toughness of HT 80

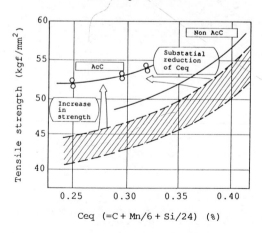

Fig.24. Relation between Ceq and strength

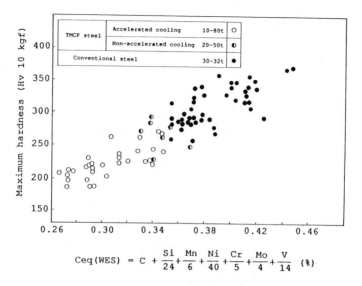

$$Ceq(WES) = C + \frac{Si}{24} + \frac{Mn}{6} + \frac{Ni}{40} + \frac{Cr}{5} + \frac{Mo}{4} + \frac{V}{14} \quad (\%)$$

Fig. 25. Effect of Ceq (WES) on maximum hardness
in the HAZ of 50 kgf/mm² class steel

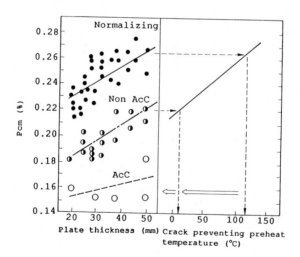

Fig. 26. Relationship between plate thickness,
weld crack preventing preheat temperature
and Pcm value for TMCP steel

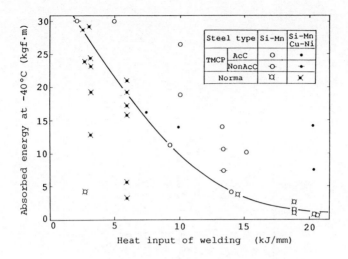

Fig. 27. Relationship between heat input of welding
and absorbed energy of most embrittled zone
in weld joint tested at -40°C

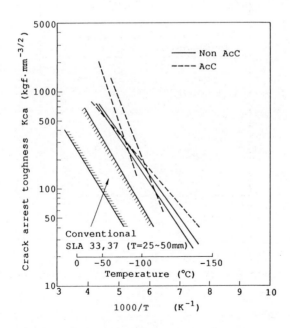

Fig. 28. ESSO or double tension test result
of Nb bearing thermo-mechanically
treated steels

1674

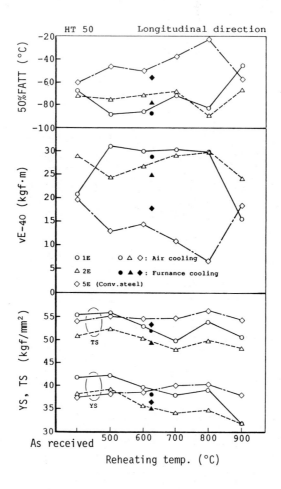

Fig. 29. Effect of reheating temperature
on mechanical properties (HT50)

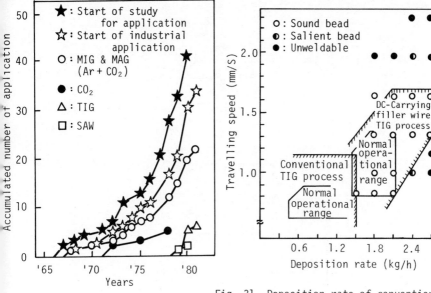

Fig.30. Growth dynamics of NGW
Accumulated number of start of
research and industrial application of NGW

Fig. 31. Deposition rate of conventional TIG
and improved TIG process

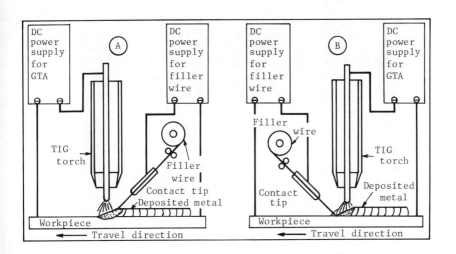

Fig. 32. Principle of MC-TIL process

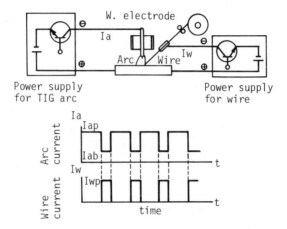

Fig. 33. Principles of HST welding process

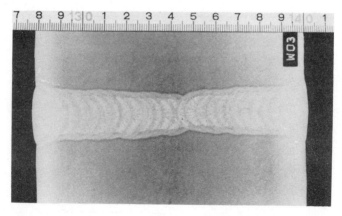

Fig. 34. Macrosection of welded joint by narrow gap SAW

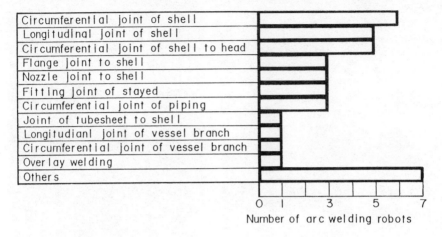

Fig. 35. Joint parts of pressure vessels and piping welded by robots in opration

Fig. 36. Large scale hanging type arc welding robot:
Welding robot manipulator for heavy section wall
(Mitsubishi Heavy Industries, Ltd.)

Fig. 37. Welding views by robot manipulator

Fig. 38. Special arc welding robot designed for branch (Mitsubishi Heavy Industris, Ltd.)

Fig. 39. Small size nozzle arc welding robot (Robot travelling type) (Kawasaki Heavy Industries, Ltd.)

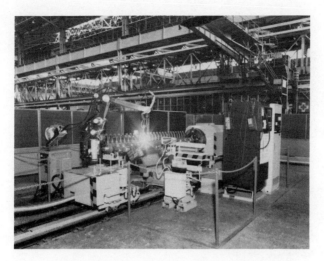

Fig. 40. Small size nozzle arc welding robot
(Work travelling type)
(Mitsubishi Heavy Industries, Ltd.)

Fig. 41. All position TIG welding robot for
pipe fixed in horizontal position
(Toshiba corp.)

Fig. 42. ESW overlay on the
reactor pressure
vessels

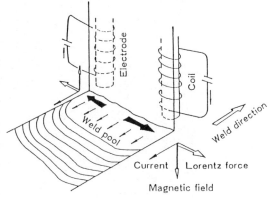

Fig. 43. Schematic illustration of induced
magnetic field

Fig. 44. Bead appearance of
ESW overlay

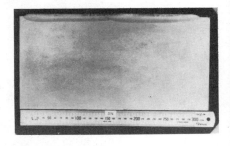

Fig. 45. Cross section of ESW overlay

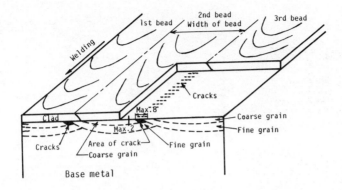

Fig. 46. Location of underclad cracking

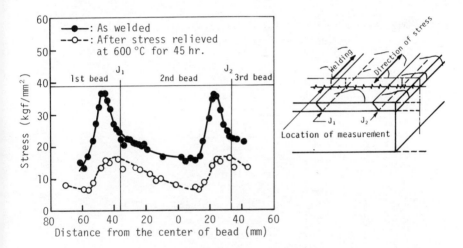

Fig. 47. Residual stress distribution in overlay welding direction

Fig. 48. Surface induction heating

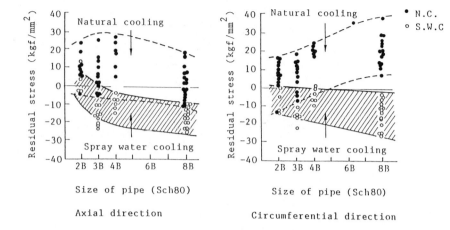

Fig. 49.   Effect of welding conditions on residual stress
of inside surface in HAZ (3 mm from fusion line)
for welded pipe

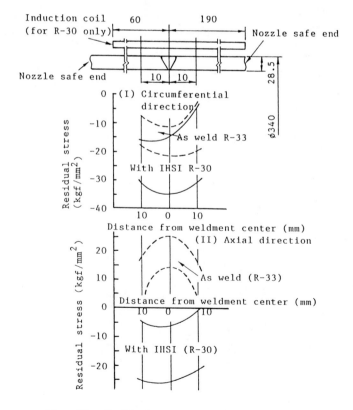

Fig. 50.   Residual stresses before and after IHSI on
an austentic stainless steel pipe weld

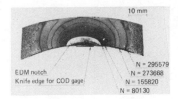 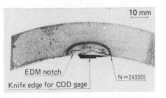

Feature surface   Fracture surface

Fig. 51. Fatigue crack growth in through thickness
direction of 8" carbon steel pipes with
and without IHSI
(Crack was arrested after a few mm growth
in the IHSI treated pipe)

Fig. 52. Setting up the induction coil for IHSI
at a Japanese BWR under construction

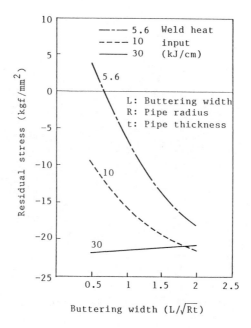

Fig. 53. Residual stress as a function
of buttering width and weld
heat input (16" dia. pipe)

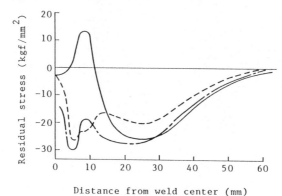

Fig. 54. Inside axial residual stress distribution
in 4" (OD.: 102 mm) pipe weldment

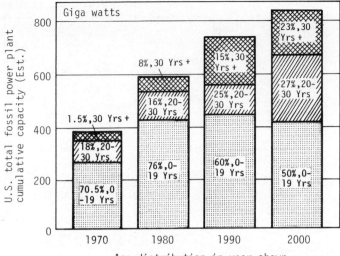

Fig. 55. Age of the U.S. electricity generating system
(Excluding nuclear)

	Testing procedures
OM	Optical microscope
SEM	Scanning electron microscope
STEM-EDX	Scanning transmission electron microscope energy dispersive X-ray spectrometer
CMA	Computer-aided microanalyser
CREEP	Creep test
SP	Small punch test
DX	X-ray diffraction

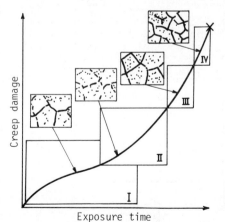

Damage parameter	Non-destructive damage detecting method
IV. Macrocracks	Visual inspection Penetrant test Magnetic particle test Ultra sonic test Radiographic test Electric resistance test
III. Microcracks	Replication method Physical test
II. Creep cavities	[Ultrasonic Electric Magnetic Radioactive]
I. Microstructural changes	Replication method Extraction replica method Physical test [Hardness X-ray diffraction] Electrochemical tests

Fig. 56. Non-destructive creep damage detection technologies
and structure analysers for damage detection

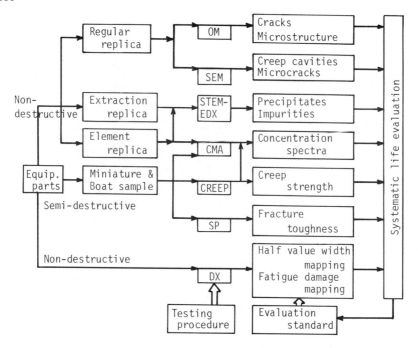

Fig. 57. Metallurgical life assessment system

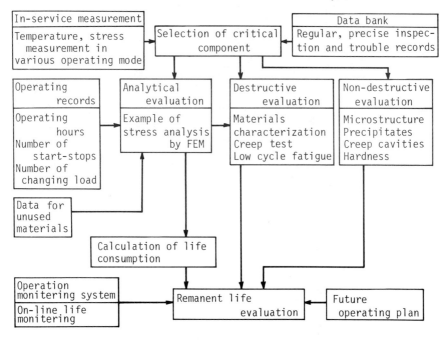

Fig. 58. Life extension system

PLENARY SESSION

Internationalization of Engineering

E. L. Daman

President, American Society of Mechanical Engineers

New York, N.Y.10017, USA

Senior Vice President, Forster Wheeler Energy Corporation

Livingston, New Jersey 07039, USA

We are living in times of unprecedented technological change--unprecedented both in scope and in the rate of change.

With this upheaval, brought about by technological advances, comes great challenges and endless opportunities for engineering innovations.

There are other forces at work in this world, such as the globalization of industry and relaxation of trade barriers. Combined with the technological thrusts I have mentioned, they present opportunities for engineers to participate in and contribute to a more stable and more integrated world community--and that is precisely what I want to talk about today.

Engineers and scientists are unique in that--regardless of nationality, religion, or race--we base our work on uniformly accepted theories and principles. In addition, engineers throughout the world have enjoyed similar technical education, greatly enhancing our ability to communicate on technical issues.

So many of the world's problems today--hunger, disease, poverty, environmental deterioration--are more amenable to solution through technological rather than political means. To that extent, we engineers have a great opportunity to work together across national borders, combining our technological skills to make this a better world for all people.

Let us first review our present state of international cooperation, and then, let us examine what we need to do to create a truly integrated world engineering community.

We are fortunate that, at least at this moment, the danger of restrictive trade practice and trade wars is on the decline--let us hope that continues. It is particularly important for the world's two greatest trading partners-- Japan and the U.S. -- to use their respective genius to stimulate world trade rather than to lapse into bilateral squabbles.

We should also be mindful of the impending unification of the European Common Market which will, by 1992, present a single market for more than 300 million people, using common standards for goods and services. The opportunities created by that event are unprecedented.

Free and open trade is essential if we hope to improve the quality of life throughout the world. We are also fortunate that the industrialized countries of the world have seen the advantage of worldwide sourcing of goods, services, and technology, thereby forging links with suppliers across national boundaries. Because of this flow of engineering, we are beginning to understand the need for uniform standards of design, safety, and quality, essential for the full exploitation of transnational operations.

Perhaps the one area where the willingness of nations to open the door wider has been restricted is technology transfer.

It is with great pride that I can state that the U.S. has a wide-open door on technology transfer—some argue, too wide. We need to find effective means to have that same open-door policy instituted in all countries of the world so that we, as a world community, can benefit from the genius and innovativeness of all cultures.

So where do we go from here?

Perhaps the most potent force moving us toward a truly integrated world-wide engineering community is the advent of computer integrated flexible manufacturing systems. Such systems, using uniform standards based on identical data bases, tolerance conventions, and quality criteria will make possible the production of identical commodities wherever such capabilities exist.

The day will come when it is routine for a project manager at my company to call a factory here in China; transmit a set of specifications for a gear, a pressure vessel, or a high-pressure valve; receive a quotation and delivery schedule; and be absolutely sure that, if purchased from the Chinese source, it will be exactly the same in terms of quality, material, dimensions and performance as a component built in the U.S., Germany, or Japan.

I am confident this will happen soon. To bring about this very exiting goal requires some hard work conducted by an international representative engineering body that must provide and agree on the adoption of standards of design, materials, and manufacturing. This group must create and adopt data bases on material properties, thermodynamic properties, other physical properties or substances, design algorithms, safety and reliability analyses, methods, and more. Later I will tell you what the ASME is trying to do to bring this about

However, the major challenge in achieving the integration we seek is in sharing technical information or, to use the well-trod words, Technology Transfer. There are still strong nationalistic protective forces that want to guard and protect technology.

I recognize that there are good reasons for rewarding the innovator; therefore, worldwide agreement on patent rights is essential and must be adopted.

Good progress has been made toward achieving adoption of such policies. We must now work hard to establish the necessary legal systems to assure full international protection for intellectual property.

We must remember that technology locked up in a box is never fully exploited. Perhaps the best case that can be made for sharing technology is to examine

what our Japanese colleagues have done in adding their great genius and
industry to foreign technology, producing ingenious equipment of high quality. But there are more compelling reasons for strong and open technology
exchange.

Our globe is a small speck in the Universe. More and more of what we do in
pursuing our communal goals is affecting the environment of this globe we
all share. We cannot continue to ignore the effect on the environment of our
industrial activity and of our parochial commercial interests.

We must find ways to come together, to pool our technology, and to attack
global environmental problems. In this respect I must confess that we in the
U.S. have not set the best of examples. Our industry says, and correctly so,
we do not fully understand the effect of sulfur, nitrogen oxides, carbon
dioxide, or other things on the environment; therefore, let us wait until
we understand that before we make changes. But yet, we know and have ample
evidence that the continuing mode of operation of industrial processes which
load the atmosphere with particulates--sulfur, NO_x, hydrocarbons, carbon
dioxide, etc.--will eventually adversely affect our environment.

Therefore, we must take action before all the scientific evidence is in.
Fortunately, there are many things we can do that will not adversely affect
the cost of what we do. For instance, in the area of my expertise, we can
take cost-effective--and I underline "cost-effective"--steps to reduce emis-
sions from power plants by raising, and raising drastically, the efficiency
of power generation. We know how to do that--we need a worldwide agreement
to implement it.

We also need to pursue the nuclear power option. We engineers know that we
can provide safe nuclear power. We must admit, however, that we have not
done a good job in providing the public with adequate, understandable, and
reliable information. Here, more than anywhere, we have to adopt international standards of design and inspection to meet our obligations vis a vis the
public.

In addition, great advances have been made and greater advances are possible
in the development of solar thermoelectric processes coupled to energy storage systems using superconducting materials technology. I cannot think of a
more fruitful field of international technical cooperation than that.

We must understand that the vast majority of the people on our globe living
in poverty desperately need to have access to adequate and cheap energy--
energy that can be supplied without further degradation of the global environment.

There are opportunities for the scientific and engineering communities world-
wide to cooperate in impending Geo-Biosphere world studies, in the Natural
Hazards studies, and in the Space Year studies--all planned in the immediate
future. Engineers need to participate in these endeavors to lead the way to
implementation of practical, cost-effective, and environmentally benign means
of energy production and industrialization.

With all this as background, the question now before us is: What can engineering societies do to move the global community toward a unified approach to
address problems that should concern all of us? That, simply stated, is the
quality of life on this, our globe.

At ASME we are trying to take a step in that direction. We have launched an initiative within ASME to form active organizations in other countries, with the explicit purpose to working with the national organization to achieve the technology transfer and to implement the standard-setting activities that are essential to the achievement of this global engineering community.

It is my hope that this initiative will be looked upon as a constructive move and not as a competitive adventure. The relationship between the ASME chapter or section in another country and the local national professional society will vary depending on the scope and organization of the professional societies in the country where ASME will have a presence.

At ASME we are determained to establish closer relationships with our colleagues around the globe by expanding our activities in technology transfer, education, and standards activities through cooperative action.

We participate in several international engineering organizations. We cosponsor research projects with a number of other countries. Under the auspices of our Board of International Affairs, we have correspondents in several countries to assist in fostering a technical information exchange among colleagues there and in the U.S.

Here are some things we could do to increase our information exchange worldwide:

(1) Establish an International Institute of Engineering Education, where engineers from different companies, at their company's expense,could be placed in overseas research laboratories or engineering companies to learn the language, the culture, and the technology of that country.

(2) Publish and disseminate uniform standards—an activity I believe vital to the achievement of a multinational engineering production system and one that offers a major role for the ASME Code and Standards operation.

(3) In countries where ASME has a chapter or section, establish technical program committees with the National Engineering Organization to encourage joint meetings for technology transfer and education.

(4) Through overseas chapters, extend ASME accreditation programs for emergin industrial processes coming into commercial operation world-wide.

(5) Participate in bilateral and multilateral studies based on local, regional, or global interest in the area of environmental or standards issues.

It is my hope that, in time, we will see the birth of a global engineering and scientific organization that is empowered to adopt uniform standards for the design and operation of engineering processes. To achieve this goal will take time. In the meantime, however, we must work together as national engineering societies to move toward that goal. That is the purpose of ASME's International Initiative.

I feel strongly that professional societies can accomplish the unification we all seek, more efficiently and much more rapidly than can the political organizations, which work through complex and powerless international umbrella organizations.

Each time we gather at an international meeting such as this, we come a step closer to understanding what a world community really means. ASME will continue its efforts to tie the world together in an engineering sense. Then, perhaps, unification in other important areas will follow--areas that will help establish a true global community while preserving the cultural differences that make the world interesting.

EUROPEAN PERSPECTIVES ON THE PREVENTION OF
CATASTROPHIC FAILURE OF PRESSURE COMPONENTS

K. KUSSMAUL
STAATLICHE MATERIALPRÜFUNGSANSTALT (MPA)
7000 STUTTGART 80
FEDERAL REPUBLIC OF GERMANY (FRG)

1. Introduction

Since the days of James Watt, pressure components have changed human life
and civilization.

Already at the beginning of this century, the invention of the high
pressure ammonia synthesis for the production of ammonium fertilizers set
new standards. The gas reaction pressure was 200 bar, the reaction
temperature ranged between 450 and 500° C; for comparison, steam boilers
operated at 10 bar and 180° C at that time. Hydrogen and ammonia turned out
to be extremely agressive to the steel boundary. The solution for the
reactor vessel was to use a ferrite liner on the inside of the pressure
vessel made of steel. Notches in the liner adjacent to the vessel wall and
drill holes through that wall provided the protection against hot hydrogen
which could escape through those channels. Even at that time, it had become
evident that materials testing is an imperative requirement and indeed
constitutes the basis for the assurance of safety and reliability.

New high pressure syntheses followed in 1922 (urea from ammonia and carbon
dioxide). The development of steel ingots up to 300 tons was associated
with the production of gigantic sizes of ingots forged in the famous Krupp
forging press with a capacity of 15 000 tons in the years 1928/30. Another
challenge of pressure vessel technology came from the high pressure
hydrogenation of coal. Since then, chemical reactors have been built which
even now represent great achievements in the fields of materials

engineering, corrosion engineering, structural engineering and integrity engineering.

We should not forget that Carl Bosch, in 1931, won the NOBEL price for his brilliant contribution to the high pressure technology of chemical reactor pressure vessels.

Some 50 years ago, his successors succeeded with the introduction of the prestressed thick-walled pressure vessel, resistant to both extremely high pressure and heavy corrosion attack. In the field of steam boilers, a breakthrough was only reached after a worldwide series of catastrophic failures of riveted boiler drums had caused more than thousand fatalities. However, experience proves that catastrophic in-service failures are still possible and have occurred even recently in spite of relatively high quality requirements, which are, nevertheless, not sufficient by themselves to make failure incredible.

Many of the sensational failures of components have initiated in weldments where embrittlement and/or cracking are most likely to occur and may create initial conditions for potential failure, especially when corrosion effects cannot be avoided.

All efforts in design, materials technology and operation conditions must therefore be directed to prevent failure of components and to quantify the safety margin as a function of time. Aging, lifetime assessment and lifetime extension become increasingly important against the background of availability, reliability and safety.

Important for chemical vessels and even more so for nuclear reactors is the following: It is an ongoing task of the engineering community to maintain pressure vessel and piping technology acceptable for the public.

Making catastrophic failure incredible was the challenge for the past 25 years of nuclear technology. It is for this reason that this paper focuses on generic issues of nuclear component safety of light water reactors (LWR), liquid metal cooled fast breeder reactors (LMFBR) and gas cooled high temperature reactors (HTR).

From the beginning of nuclear technology, a very cautious approach has been adopted in relation to the prevention of catastrophic failure of pressure boundary components and especially of pressure vessels and tanks.

Two general arguments have been put forward to give safety assurance:

- Integrity is achieved by design, manufacture, inspection and testing in such a way that the possibility of disruptive failure without forewarning is sufficiently remote as to be deemed incredible.
- Pressure vessel safety is demonstrated by a mechanistic–deterministic evaluation through analysis and testing to show that the sizes of defects which are of safety concern are large in relation to those which may be present in the component, even under worst case conditions.

Safe and economic operation is possible on the basis of existing regulations and design principles. However, the improvement of nuclear power plant design and materials technology, including quality assurance, control and monitoring during operation, and repeated inspection, is an important prerequisite, if safety and reliability are to be guaranteed also in the future. In Europe, the engineering community constantly strives to improve and does not feel that there is an imaginary plateau of technology where one can rest /1/.

2. Probabilistic Approach

According to probabilistic investigations, the probability of catastrophic failure of pressure vessels of nuclear power plants is very low. Low levels of 10^{-7} to 10^{-10} per reactor year emphasize the unlikeliness of a catastrophe, but they do not in principle exclude it mathematically; a risk remains.

The following restrictions and limits exist for probabilistic methods:

- Experience with nuclear vessels is not sufficient to provide a useful direct estimate of the failure probability. There are not enough reactor-years of operation to use the classical methods of statistics, since the population sample available is not statistically significant at the low levels of probability expected to derive.
- There is no satisfactory way of interpreting the data on potential failure rates for conventional vessels to give a useful estimate of the possible catastrophic failure rate of nuclear pressure vessels.
- Although a synthesis of vessel failure probability can be constructed, it relies on assumptions which cannot be validated, for example, on the

distribution of defects. Human error has to be considered. The state of the international data base including the crack pattern and the scatter in the fracture mechanics characteristics is not yet sufficently established.

Probabilistic methods can at best give an idea of the magnitude of catastrophic.failure probability. No reliance can be placed on the absolute levels of the numbers derived in this way. Nevertheless, probabilistic analysis does play a role, primarily as a tool to compare different designs and to evaluate areas of weakness in structural integrity. Probabilistic methods are not a sufficient basis for catastrophic failure exclusion.

To demonstrate that the possibility of catastrophic failure is completely excluded, it is necessary to implement the mechanistic/deterministic analysis.

3. Basis Safety Concept

Basis safety /2/, Fig. 1, is attained through measures enhancing quality ("quality through production" principle). This comprises optimization of style of the component, selection of improved ferritic and austenitic materials, advanced manufacturing with stringent and well-documented process control and qualification. The design is based on loading parameters resulting from normal operation as well as upset, emergency and faulted conditions. The integrity of components and systems is assured through high toughness, minimized defect formation and low levels of working stresses. Basis safety has the aim of preventing failure. It is thus a primary safety measure.

The basis safety which alone suffices to give assurance against catastrophic failure requires the existence of enough redundancies to ensure that any possible departure from optimization is sufficiently unimportant. It is the provision of such redundancies which constitutes the essence of the Basis Safety Concept. This strategy provides a sufficiently large safety margin even if there is no guarantee for a 100% effectiveness of each single redundancy. With the Basis Safety Concept it is essential to assess integrity in a mechanistic/deterministic way without invoking probabilistic argument and despite human error. The key issue is the choice and specification of improved materials manufactured and processed with regard to cleanness, homogeneity, isotropy, strength, toughness, corrosion and erosion resistance. This is imperative for plant performance as well as advanced manufacturing and improved design for all safety-related components.

In essence, the optimum style for the reactor presssure vessel consists of combining the flange and nozzle parts into one single, smooth, highly reinforced ring with large ligaments between the nozzle penetrations and set-on nozzles, using separate supports for the vessel, Fig. 2. The set-on nozzle has practically no load-bearing function. The resulting monolithic structure is superior to a composite structure with through-wall nozzle weldments of conventional design. A thicker nozzle belt reduces flange rotation and hence bending stresses. Simplified shapes with long parallel-sided sections adjacent to the welds ease the inspectability and improve tandemprobe inspection.

Integral nozzle shell style, of which the cross section is shown in Fig. 3, has been a feature of 20 water reactor pressure vessels supplied by a German vendor, including a giant vessel, Figs. 4 and 5. Some integral vessels have also been designed by a foreign manufacturer from Europe and fabricated accordingly.

Materials and Manufacturing

A significant feature in the development of reactor pressure boundary steels and welding techniques for reactor components has been the increase in maximum ingot size for the forged rings of the pressure vessel. The size has ranged from 220t to 570t in the past 20 years using advanced forging technology. The increasing size of the forged rings made it possible to build pressure vessels of increasing dimensions and, at the same time, to reduce the number of welds.

In addition, the narrow gap welding technology proved to be advantageous compared to the usual procedure, Fig. 5.

The structural integrity of the components of light water reactors is decisively controlled by the toughness of the material, Fig. 6. Therefore, an important feature, which has accompanied the improvements in steelmaking practice, has been the continuous optimization of quality with regard to homogeneity, isotropy and fracture toughness. An important prerequisite for structural materials application is their suitability for welding, since welding may increase the susceptibility to heat affected zone embrittlement and cracking as well as to sensitization for corrosion attack possibly leading to serious transgranular or intergranular stress corrosion cracking.

By introducing suitable materials with balanced alloying elements and a very low content of accompanying and trace elements, it has been possible to control the phenomenon of embrittlement and cracking in the heat-affected zone of weldments. A high degree of purity and a limitation on segregation is one decisive prerequisite for the aging performance of the materials.

Components of high purity, homogeneity and isotropy without any macro-segregations and with extraordinary high strength and toughness uniform across the wall thickness can be manufactured by "shape welding" /3/. Thick-walled components of any dimensions and complex shape are built up by the submerged arc welding process. The example given here is that of an hydrocracker, Fig. 7. In addition, branches and even elbows have been manufactured by shape welding. However, due to the high manufacturing costs, there is no break-through of this promising development.

Independent Redundancies

As mentioned above, a reliable Safety Concept requires enough redundancies to reinforce the assurance against catastrophic failure, Fig. 1. The first redundancy is provided by having the initial component integrity verified by a number of independent quality assurance programmes. This constitutes the principle "multiple party testing".

A second and crucial redundancy is furnished by the demonstration that there is a worst state below which the condition of the material cannot fall: this is the "worst case principle". The necessary assurance is provided by defect and failure investigations to establish the mechanism and possible extent of degradation through manufacturing and operational aging, Figs. 8 and 9. As far as possible, plant aging is being considered at the design stage, taking appropriate steps to cope with the potential aging mechanisms. Corrosion effects on the materials may exhaust dramatically both static and cyclic loading capacity. This becomes even more critical when flow induced erosion is occuring. Irradiation or creep embrittlement with interaction of the coolant and the stresses may occur in the RPVs respectively the reactor tanks and the high temperature piping. To assess the worst case performance of material, it is essential to have available not only parts deliberately manufactured with artificial defects, but also rejects occurring in the ordinary process of manufacture to quantify the safety margin for lower bound conditions.

A third redundancy in the Basis Safety Concept consists of in-service verifications so that design conditions are not exceeded during plant operation ("in-service monitoring and documentation principle"). This guarantees that the design is conservative in relation to the service conditions it encounters, Fig. 10.

Due to the special significance attached to non-destructive testing techniques, considerable interest is centred on this subject. Advanced non-destructive testing techniques provide improved flaw detection and sizing /4/, Fig. 11. The automation of testing has brought about a significant reduction in inspection times and in radiation exposures received by the personnel. For example, all important locations of the primary circuit of a LWR have been instrumented to monitor and analyze the state of the given system.

The fourth redundancy is the "validation principle" which relies on the verification and validation of calculation codes and mechanistic fracture mechanics as well as probabilistic evaluation of non-destructive examination methods.

Validation

There is no better way to validate and to quantify the capability of remote testing techniques for in-service inspection than by using full-scale components, containing all representative kinds of natural and artificial flaws /5/.

The full-scale validation trials must include the complete electronics and data processing systems as well as examining the training programmes for the personnel /2/. Fig. 12 shows the heart of the NDE validation centre at MPA Stuttgart: a full-size vessel combining typical structures of boiling and pressurized water reactors. The most upper ring with inserts of various types of set-on and set-in nozzles in the shell section representing the flange ring of a PWR is used for the international NDE-research programme

PISC III (Programme for the Inspection of Steel Components) in which 10 European countries participate together with USA and Japan. At present this programme concentrates on ultrasonic full volumetric examination /6, 7/. Additional programmes deal with the evaluation of acoustic emission. In Fig. 13 a view from above with the central mast manipulator gives an idea of the equipment.

Additional inspection validation centres in Europe using full-scale components and mock-ups are located for example in Great Britain and France /8, 9, 10/, Figs. 14 and 15.
The validation of constructive materials laws, stress and fracture mechanics calculations and the corresponding computer codes is obtained through the testing of both small-scale and large-scale specimens, Fig. 16, and components /11/. To simulate the impacts from hazards such as water hammer, earthquake and aircraft crash on the primary coolant circuit and safety protection systems as well as energy excursion events like the Bethe-Tait event in LMFBRs, large-scale testing facilities for static and high speed loading are necessary. Outstanding testing facilities can be found in several European countries, either ready for testing or under construction, Figs. 17 to 19.
For the validation of the existing concepts for stress-strain calculation (computer codes) and fracture mechanics concepts, pressurized thermal shock (PTS) analysis and testing is the most suitable example, since it produces the most complex and at the same time critical loading situation in a component. For this reason great effort has been placed in this field and suitable testing facilities have been installed, Figs. 20 to 23. Crack extension and failure occurrence can be predicted on the basis of the well-developed fracture mechanics parameters considering the constraint in the ligament.

4. Application of the Basis Safety Concept for Piping

For austenitic structural steels of piping different approaches are used. An important issue is whether or not to use stabilized or non-stabilized materials. The first commercial BWR in Germany was built with primary piping made of unstabilized austenitic steel according to the philosophy of the American nuclear vendor. Due to the predicted problem of intergranular corrosion, the next step was to insist on the sole use of stabilized austenitic material. Further development led to high toughness ferritic seamless straight pipes with internal austenitic cladding instead of cast austenitic piping which have several advantages especially that of ultrasonic testing feasibility. Large 180° elbows for reactor coolant piping (PWR), Fig. 24, have formerly been manufactured from pressed semi-shells with longitudinal weldments and internal austenitic strip cladding (I.D. = 965 mm). Seamless elbows and pipe bends are now produced by inductive bending.

For primary coolant piping, the number of welds has been reduced drastically, from 250 in older plants to 60 in more recent ones, by advanced design, forging and inductive bending technology, Fig. 25. Full-scale verification testing under operational conditions gave confidence in the improvements.

The assessment of leak-before-catastrophic-failure is based upon numerous tests on tubes, pipes and vessels as well as failure analysis.

Generally, the investigations on the effect of flaws of pressurized cylindrical components are first and foremost carried out using longitudinal flaws (flaw perpendicular to the maximum stress under internal pressure).

In the field of piping however, straight pipes with longitudinal flaws exposed to internal pressure were only the first stage of extensive research programmes on vessel failure. The next stages include

- other components
  . elbows
  . forged pieces

- complex loading
  . internal pressure and superimposed outer bending moment (static, cyclic, dynamic, impact)
  . temperature and corrosive agent

- other kinds of defects
  . circumferential flaws (representative also for welding defects on circumferential welds).

Tremendous efforts have been made to cope with these problems in several

1704

European countries with national and international programmes. The results
of the research projects can be summarized as follows:

- The load bearing capacity of pipes affected by longitudinal or
  circumferential defects can be determined.

- The leak–before–break curve as a boundary between the formation of
  leakage and catastrophic failure depends on the toughness of the
  material.

- The allowable loading and energy absorption decreases with increasing
  flaw length.

- The critical flaw length becomes smaller as the bending moment increases,
  assuming a constant nominal stress level.

It can be shown that the size of defect which might not be detected by NDE
is smaller than the size of defect which could become critical even under
faulted conditions. Nevertheless, the application of the basis safety
system which comprises the exclusion of catastrophic failure has to be
examined on a case–by–case basis for individual plants.

5. Aging

The potential in–service aging mechanisms for primary components of LWRs
and the resulting effects on materials and components are shown
schematically in the Figs. 8 and 9.
Problems of corrosion including crack corrosion and erosion corrosion
through wear can be resolved by the use of appropriate materials and a
controlled water chemistry. The regulations of several European countries
include the requirement that the resistance against corrosive attack of
qualified material and the risk of corrosion during operation has to be
verified. In autoclave systems and in operating LWRs, the interaction of
temperature, cyclic loading, coolant corrosion and even irradiation is
investigated. By such research programmes, adequate knowledge about the
long–term behaviour is provided in time.

The results of material examination programmes on long–term behaviour confirm that an operational change of resistance follows known physical and physical/chemical laws. Thus failure is impossible without a previous sign of warning. Through examination and monitoring during operation and through accompanying research programmes all material degradations and changes of the plant are recognized reliably and timely. In the worst case, decisions on continued operation or on the exchange of components have to be made without too much time in between. Large and costly exchanges due to degradation have been made especially in piping systems and steam generators.

6. Safety Concepts for Advanced Reactor Types

The same stringent approach as described for light water reactors is adopted for gas cooled HTRs and sodium cooled FBRs, not only for the primary circuit components but also for those of the water/steam circuit.

This can be illustrated by what is called R&D programme MINERVA, Fig. 26, which is concentrating on dissimilar welds for HTR-application. The qualification of the dissimilar welds is evaluated on full-scale components under internal pressure at the relevant temperatures up to 550°C with a total test time of 20 000 h. The structural integrity of components in the elevated and high temperature regime is investigated in European research and development programmes comprising

- creep relaxation, creep-fatigue, creep-ratcheting on piping, elbows, shell-plate junctions,

- buckling of thin shells, thermal striping

- cyclic thermal shock.

Other European research activities in connection with advanced reactors concentrate on crack growth evaluation and the validation of computer codes. Examples of joint European R&D programmes focused on FBRs proved the effectiveness of an open and friendly way to cooperate.

7. Conclusions

From the experience obtained from conventional power plants and from the numerous pressure vessels in the chemical industry it was possible to specify requirements which provided a basis for the prevention of catastrophic failure of pressure components. In the past, concerns about the safety of nuclear power plants have led to a world-wide enhancement of the research activities. The continuing efforts of the nuclear community in Europe add to the understanding of integrity engineering in all important fields of technology. The Basis Safety Concept allows catastrophic failure to be excluded by a deterministic/mechanistic analysis. It can be seen, without detailed calculation and despite human errors, that failure probabilities are so low as to be meaningless. According to the Basis Safety Concept, the safety margin is large enough to justify the assumption of incredibility of catastrophic failure.

References

/1/ Kussmaul, K., Herter, K.-H. and Baugé, S.
    Comparison of Safety Requirements of the Primary Pressure Boundary in Safety Standards of the Federal Republic of Germany, France and Other Countries
    IAEA-SM-307/10, Nov. 1988

/2/ Kussmaul, K.
    German Basis Safety Concept Rules out Possibility of Catastrophic Failure
    Nuclear Engineering International, Dec. 1984, pp. 41/46

/3/ Kussmaul, K., Schoch, F.-W. and Luckow, H.
    High Quality Large Components "Shape Welded" by a SAW Process
    Welding Journal, Sept. 1983, pp. 17/24

/4/ Streicher, V. and Miksch, M.
    KWU's Series '86 Systems Increase Life Expectancy, Availability and Safety
    Nuclear Engineering International, March 1988, pp. 27/33

/5/ Aufgaben, Ziele und erste Ergebnisse des Forschungsprogramms Komponentensicherheit
    Tasks, Aims and First Results of the Research Programme Component Safety
    VGB Kraftwerkstechnik 60 (1980) No. 6, pp. 438/49

/6/ Kussmaul, K., Mletzko, U. and Sturm, D.
    Automatic In-Service-Inspection of a BWR Pressure Vessel with Additional PWR Moduels - FSV Activities of the PISC III Programme -
    ICPVT-6, Beijing, Sept. 1988

/7/ Crutzen, S. et al.
PISC Full Scale Reactor Pressure Vessel Validation of Non-Destructive
Examination
14th MPA-Seminar Safety and Reliability of Plant Technology,
Stuttgart, Oct. 1988
to be published in the International Journal of Nuclear Engineering
and Design

/8/ C.E.T.I.C.
Maintenance Preparation and Qualification Center for PWR Nuclear Steam
Supply Systems
C.E.T.I.C. Publication

/9/ Gardner, W. E. and Whittle, M. J.
Advances Arising from the UK PWR Programme in the Detection and Sizing
of Defects
12th MPA-Seminar Safety and Reliability of Plant Technology,
Stuttgart, Oct. 1986
see also
Gardner, W. E. and Darlaston, B. J.
Advances in PWR Structural Integrity Assessment and Materials
Technology in the United Kingdom
Nuclear Engineering and Design, Vol. 102 (1987) No. 3, July 1987, pp.
419/430

/10/ Cartwright, D. K.
Validation of the Inspection of PWR Pressure Vessels
Atom No. 367, May 1987, pp. 2/4

/11/ Tomkins, B.
The Structural Integrity Centre
Atom No. 367, May 1987, pp. 4/8

1708

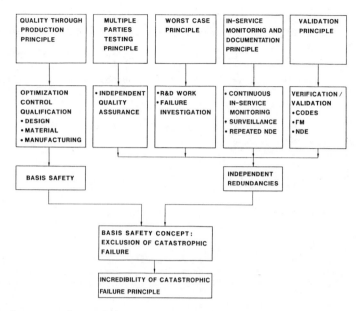

<u>Fig. 1:</u>   Basis Safety Concept and
         incredibility-of-catastrophic-failure principle.

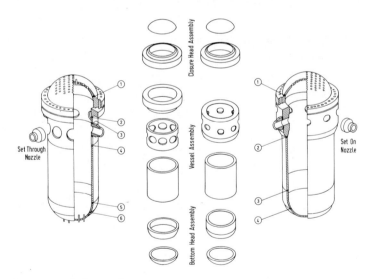

<u>Fig. 2:</u>   Examples of Reactor Pressure Vessel (RPV) style for
         4-loop Pressurized Water Reactor.

         left: conventional style with set-through
              nozzles.

         right: advanced "integral" style with set-on
              nozzles.

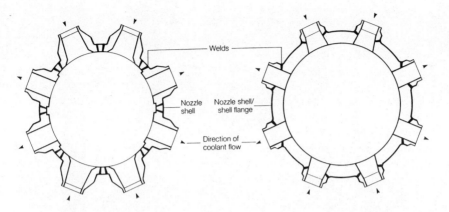

Fig. 3: Cross sections of Reactor Pressure Vessels in Fig. 2.

left: conventional style with set-through nozzles.

right: advanced "integral" style with set-on nozzles.

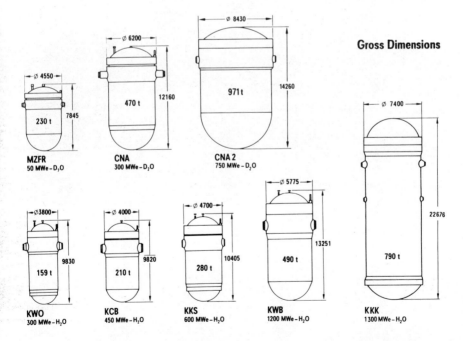

Fig. 4: Gross dimensions of Reactor Pressure Vessels of Presssurized and Boiling Water Reactors, executed orders in the FRG.

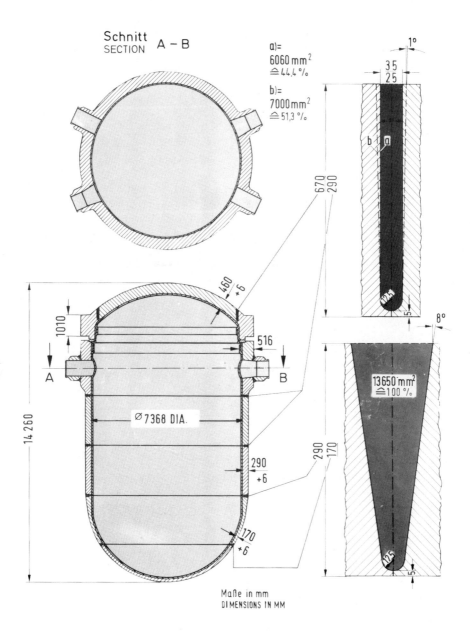

Schnitt A – B
SECTION

a)= 6060 mm²
≙ 44,4 %

b)= 7000 mm²
≙ 51,3 %

460 +6

516

1010

A   B

Ø 7368 DIA.

14 260

290 +6

170 +6

670   290

290   170

13650 mm²
≙ 100 %

1°

35
25

b a

125

5

8°

125

5

Maße in mm
DIMENSIONS IN MM

Fig. 5:   971t Reactor Pressure Vessel of a 700 MWe Heavy Water Reactor with narrow gap welds up to 670 mm thickness.

BASIS SAFETY CONCEPT - MATERIALS

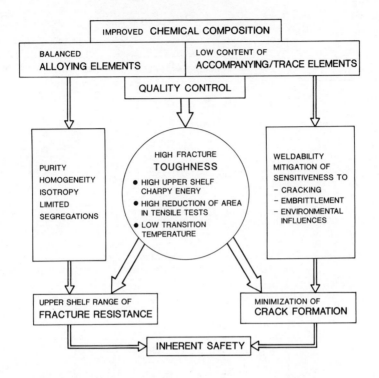

Fig. 6:   Basis Safety Concept for materials.

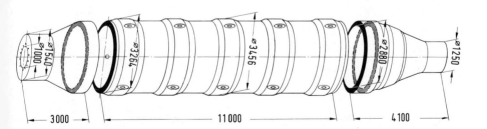

Fig. 7:   200t Hydrocracker manufactured by shape welding.

	TEMPERATURE					
		NEUTRON FLUX	LOAD: STATIC, CYCLIC, DYNAMIC		RELATIVE MOTION	
				LIQUID MEDIUM		
	THERMAL AGEING	IRRADIATION	CREEP	FATIGUE	CORROSION	WEAR
REDUCTION OF TOUGHNESS	●	●	●			
GRAIN DISINTEGRATION					●	
CRACKING			●	● ● ●	●	
PITTING					●	● ●
SWELLING		●				
THINNING					●	● ●
DENTING					●	

IN-SERVICE AGEING — POTENTIAL EFFECTS ON MATERIALS AND COMPONENTS

Fig. 8: Parameters relevant for in-service aging potential of materials and components.

	TEMPERATURE					
		NEUTRON FLUX	LOAD: STATIC, CYCLIC, DYNAMIC		RELATIVE MOTION	
				LIQUID MEDIUM		
	THERMAL AGEING	IRRADIATION	CREEP	FATIGUE	CORROSION	WEAR
RPV VESSEL SHELL	○	●		○	○	
FUEL ELEMENT CLADDING	○	○	○	○	●	
SG VESSEL SHELL				○	○	○
SG TUBES				○	●	○
MAIN COOLANT PIPING				○	○	
MAIN COOLANT PUMP				●	○	
FEED WATER / WET STEAM PIPING				○	●	●
TURBINE				●	○	●
CONDENSATOR TUBES				○	●	

○ POTENTIAL AGEING MECHANISM   ● LEADING AGEING MECHANISM

Fig. 9: In-service aging mechanisms of typical light water reactor components.

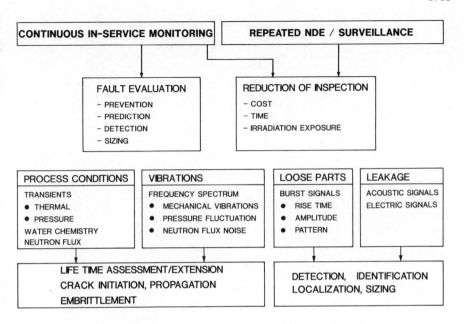

| CONTINUOUS IN-SERVICE MONITORING | REPEATED NDE / SURVEILLANCE |

FAULT EVALUATION	REDUCTION OF INSPECTION
– PREVENTION	– COST
– PREDICTION	– TIME
– DETECTION	– IRRADIATION EXPOSURE
– SIZING	

PROCESS CONDITIONS	VIBRATIONS	LOOSE PARTS	LEAKAGE
TRANSIENTS	FREQUENCY SPECTRUM	BURST SIGNALS	ACOUSTIC SIGNALS
● THERMAL	● MECHANICAL VIBRATIONS	● RISE TIME	ELECTRIC SIGNALS
● PRESSURE	● PRESSURE FLUCTUATION	● AMPLITUDE	
WATER CHEMISTRY	● NEUTRON FLUX NOISE	● PATTERN	
NEUTRON FLUX			

| LIFE TIME ASSESSMENT/EXTENSION CRACK INITIATION, PROPAGATION EMBRITTLEMENT | DETECTION, IDENTIFICATION LOCALIZATION, SIZING |

Fig. 10: Basis Safety Concept: In-service monitoring principle, monitoring and detection systems.

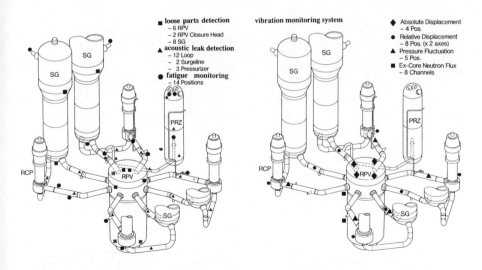

Fig. 11: On-line monitoring and diagnostics in the primary circuit of Pressurized Water Reactors (acc. to Streicher et al.).

1714

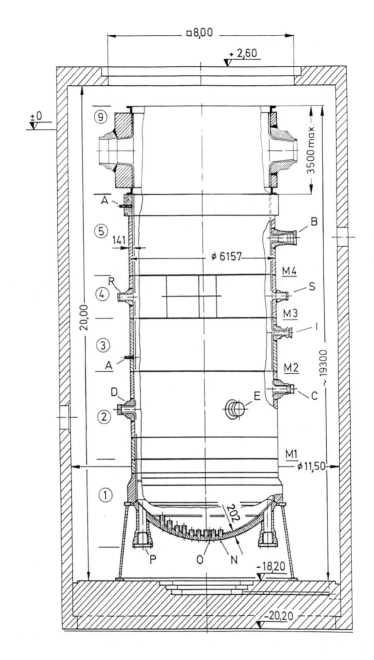

Fig. 12: Non-destructive examination validation centre at MPA Stuttgart. Full-size reactor pressure vessel (900 MW$_e$ BWR) with additional PWR module (position 9) for housing 900, 1200, 1300 MW$_e$ reactor nozzle plates

Fig. 13: Central mast manipulator to be used in the full size reactor pressure vessel installed at MPA Stuttgart, FRG.

Fig. 14: Steam generator mock-up for NDE-qualification.
Maintenance Preparation and Qualification Center
for PWR Nuclear Steam Supply Systems (C.E.T.I.C.),
Chalons-sur-Saone (France).

Fig. 15: Ultrasonic inspection of pressure vessel weld test assembly in the Inspection Validation Centre (IVC) at the Risley Nuclear Laboratories, UK.

1718

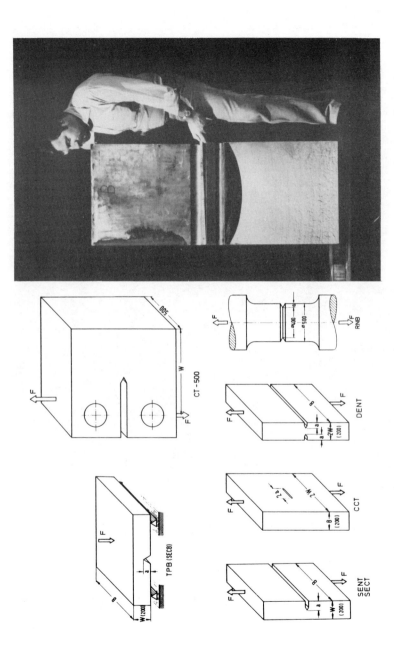

Fig. 16: Large-scale test specimen for the validation of fracture mechanics used at MPA Stuttgart, FRG.

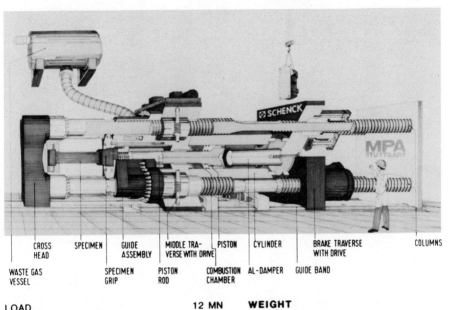

CROSS HEAD	SPECIMEN	GUIDE ASSEMBLY

CROSS HEAD	SPECIMEN	GUIDE ASSEMBLY	MIDDLE TRA- VERSE WITH DRIVE	PISTON	CYLINDER	BRAKE TRAVERSE WITH DRIVE	COLUMNS
WASTE GAS VESSEL		SPECIMEN GRIP	PISTON ROD	COMBUSTION CHAMBER	AL-DAMPER	GUIDE BAND	

LOAD	12 MN	**WEIGHT**		
STROKE	600 (1300) mm	TOTAL	490 t	
VELOCITY		ACCELERATING PARTS	15 t	
-AFTER 20 mm STROKE	25 m/s	ACCELERATION FORCE		
-AFTER 400 mm STROKE	60 m/s		100 MN	
LOAD FRAME STIFFNESS	10^{10} N/m			
CROSS-SECTIONAL AREA	20000 mm^2	**STRESSES**		
MAX. INTERNAL PRESSURE	200 MPa	PISTON ROD	MAX. 900 MPa	
I.D. OF CYLINDER	1200 mm	CYLINDER	MAX. 625 MPa	

Fig. 17: High capacity dynamic tensile testing machine with gunpowder as propellant installed at MPA Stuttgart, FRG.

Structural Integrity Centre, Risley

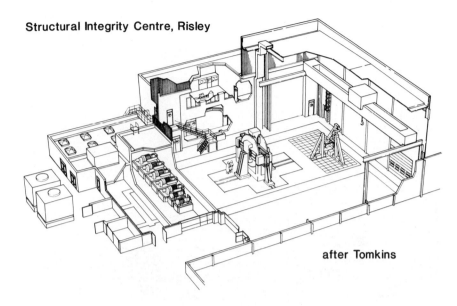

after Tomkins

Fig. 18: Structural Integrity Centre, UKAEA Risley Laboratories, UK.

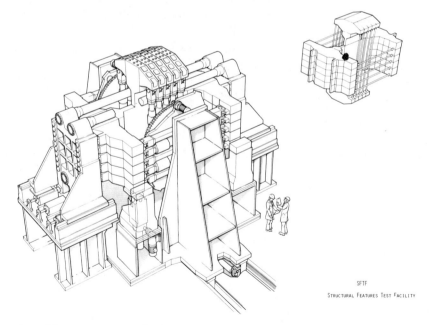

Fig. 19: Structural features test facility with 10 000 tons loading capacity in the "distributed loading technique" under construction at UKAEA Risley Laboratories, UK.

JRC Ispra PTS
(Pressurized Thermal Shock)

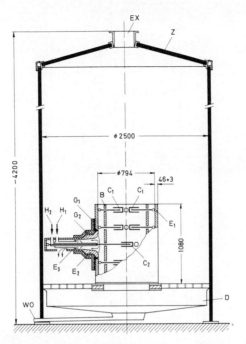

Fig. 20: Pressurized thermal shock experiment with nozzle corner cracks at the CEC Joint Research Center (JRC), Ispra, Italy.

JRC Ispra PTS experiment cooling device

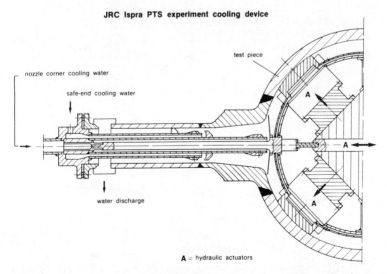

Fig. 21: JRC Ispra PTS experiment cooling device

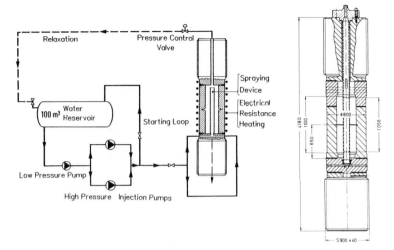

Fig. 22:   MPA thermal shock trial for experiments on
            thick-walled hollow cylinders.

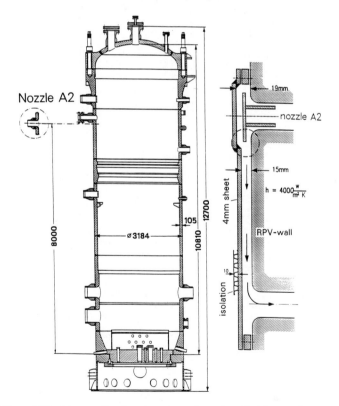

Fig. 23:   HDR thermal shock experiment, full-scale reactor
            pressure vessel with cooling device; HDR Plant, FRG

Fig. 24: 180° elbow, diameter 965 mm, with internal
austenitic strip cladding. Reactor coolant piping
(PWR).

1724

Reactor Coolant Piping

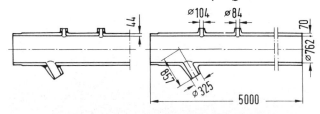

conventional	technology	advanced
	REDUCTION OF NUMBER OF	
60	Circumferential welds to	60
48	Longitudinal welds to	0
16	Nozzle welds to	0
113	Nozzle reinforcements to	0
237	Total number of welds	60

Fig. 25: Reactor coolant piping of a 4-loop PWR. Reduction in number of welds by advanced design.

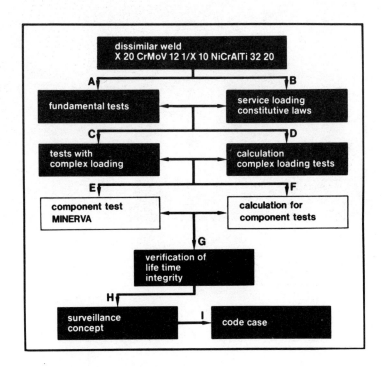

Fig. 26: Research and development program MINERVA for dissimilar weld in the high temperature range; ASEA Brown Boveri, FRG.

PROGRESS OF PRESSURE VESSEL TECHNOLOGY
IN THE PEOPLE'S REPUBLIC OF CHINA

Cengdian Liu

President, Chinese Pressure Vessel Institution
Hefei, Anhui, People's Republic of China

Chief Engineer, General Machinery Research Institute
Hefei, Anhui, People's Republic of China

ABSTRACT

This paper reviews the progress of pressure vessel technology which has been made in China since the birth of the People's Republic of China in 1949. Major development of high pressure vessels, pressure vessels for special purposes, materials for making pressure vessels and pressure vessel codes are discussed.

KEYWORDS

Flat steel ribbon wound vessel; high pressure vessel; low alloyed steel; National Standard (GB); PWR; Professional Standard (ZB); Superhigh pressure vessel; titanium.

INTRODUCTION

Pressure vessels are widely used in many branches of industries, such as chemical, petro-chemical, energy resources, etc. At the birth of the People's Republic of China in 1949, there were only facilities fabricating pressure vessels of low pressure range, the national total annual production then being less than 200 tons. To meet the basic necessities of her heavy population, the P.R. of China has developed her own chemical, petro-chemical and energy resources industries enormously during the past forty years, which has in turn enhanced the technical aspects of her pressure vessel industry. At present China is already in a position to fabricate by herself pressure vessels of different categories to meet her own demands. Based on the statistical data, the number of pressure vessels now in operation in China amounts to approximately one million, not counting portable ones. It is the purpose of the present paper to give a brief introductory statement on the developments of pressure vessels now in operation in China's important

branches of industries, including those designed and fabricated for special
purpose, and on the developments of materials for making pressure vessels,
of methods of fabrication as well as developments in relevant design and
fabrication codes and standards compiled specially for pressure vessels.

HIGH PRESSURE VESSELS

Although China was already capable of fabricating medium- and low-pressure
vessels during the early fifties, large-sized vessels and high pressure
vessels were mainly imported from the USSR. In 1956, in order to satisfy the
requirements of equipment in establishing the first synthetic ammonia plant
of China's own design, with a production capacity of 25,000 tons NH_3/year,
China started to build up her own fabricators of large-sized pressure vessels. In the same year, a prototype high pressure vessel was turned out by
the Nanjing Chemical Machinery Works, the rated pressure of the prototype
vessel being 32 MPa. The vessel was of the manually welded multilayer construction. The bursting test on the vessel was satisfactory. In 1958,
another prototype vessel of submerged arc welded multilayer construction,
with a designed pressure of 32 MPa, was turned out by the Harbin Boiler
Works. It also passed the bursting test successfully (Liu, 1959). The relevant data of the two prototype vessels are shown in Table 1.

TABLE 1   Test Data of Multilayer Prototype High Pressure Vessels

Welding process	Inside diameter (mm)	Wall thickness (mm)	Bursting pressure (MPa)	Steel inner core	Steel layer plates
Manual arc welding	584	112	126.5	20g*	G3*
Submerged arc welding	800	169	153	20g	20g

*NOTES   20g and G3 are Chinese grade of mild steels

Fig. 1.   The submerged arc welded multilayer prototype
high pressure vessel after bursting test

Figure 1 shows a view of the prototype high pressure vessel made by sub-merged arc welding, taken immediately after bursting. Batches of multilayer high pressure vessels were turned out from the fabricators in China there-after.

In the early sixties, the rapid growth of China's agriculture needed tremen-dous amount of chemical fertilizer, especially the nitrogen fertilizer,which enhanced the establishment of more than one thousand small-sized synthetic ammonia plants in most districts of China. Their production capacities were in the ranges of 3000 to 5000 tons NH_3/year. Such a situation demanded the supply of large quantites of high pressure vessels.Although the sizes of the vessels were small, yet it was desirable that they should be easily fabri-cated and they must show guaranteed of safety under operating conditions. To meet such an urgent need, the Zhejiang University and the General Machin-ery Research Institute in cooperation with the Nanjing Chemical Machinery No.2 Works successfully turned out a new unique type of flat ribbon wound high pressure vessel, after a painstaking period of trial-production (Bao and others, 1987). The new type vessel is different from the traditional, interlocking ribbon wound high pressure vessels in that the flat steel ribbon used for the new type vessel has a cross-section of rectangular shape, without grooves on the ribbon surfaces. The flat steel ribbon wound in layers over the core vessel are capable of standing the axial loads. This is because the inclinations of adjacent layers are just in opposite directions. As the investment cost for the flat steel ribbon is low and the operating cost to wind is also low, the overall cost of this type of high pressure vessel is lower than the costs of the other types. One vessel of this type with a designed pressure of 32 MPa and inside diameter of 500 mm and with nozzles connected on passed the bursting test satisfactorily, the test data of which are shown in Table 2. Figure 2 shows a view of this vessel after the bursting test.

TABLE 2   Test Data for the Prototype Flat Steel Ribbon
Wound High Pressure Vessel

Inside diameter (mm)	Wall thickness of inner core (mm)	Thickness of layers (mm)	Total wall thickness (mm)	Bursting pressure (MPa)	Material	
					Inner core	Steel ribbon
500	16	48	64	114	20g	16Mn[*]

[*]NOTES   16Mn is the Chinese grade of C-Mn steel

Many bursting tests were carried out on this new type of high pressure vessels; among the vessels tested, the biggest inside diameter was 1 meter. The test results indicated that the new type vessel possessed enough axial strength, and that there is an ample margin of safety in their use.

1728

Fig. 2. A view of the prototype flat steel ribbon wound
high pressure vessel after the bursting test.

Up to the present, there are approximately 5,000 vessels of this type now
in operation in China with a maximum working pressure of 32 MPa, a maximum
inside diameter of 1 meter, a maximum wall thickness of 150 mm, a maximum
number of wound layers of 28, and a maximum length of vessel 22 meters.

In the early seventies, with a view of improving the unit energy consumption
China started to design and install large-sized synthetic ammonia plants,
the production capacity of each unit being 300,000 tons NH_3/year. The
reactor vessel used in this design for the synthesis of NH_3 from nitrogen
and hydrogen had an inside diameter of 3,200 mm, a wall thickness of 150 mm.
At that time, China was still incapable of producing alloyed steel plates
of such thickness and therefore it was decided to forego the use of solid-
wall rolled plate construction. Moreover the multilayer construction used
previously was also impractical because such a method need a long period of
fabrication and had only a low production efficiency because of unwieldiness.
After a period of trial-production, it was decided to use the cylindrical
multiwall, shrink-fit construction for the vessel needed. The vessel was
composed of three concentric cylinders of 18MnMoNbR alloyed steel plates of
50 mm thick, telescoped together under hot conditions. The 18MnMoNbR alloyed
steel plates used were heat-treated before fabrication by normalising plus
tempering. The yield strength and tensile strength of the heat-treated
plates were both higher than the 16Mn steel plates used for the wrapped multilayer construction. Therefore the weight of the resulting vessel was lower
(Bao and others, 1987). Table 3 shows the technical parameters of an ammonia
synthesis reactor vessel with a production capacity of 300,000 tons NH_3/year,
which was fabricated by the Shanghai Boiler Works. Figure 3 shows the
appearance of this vessel.

TABLE 3   Technical Parameters of a 300,000 Tons NH_3/year
Ammonia Synthesis Reactor Vessel

Inside diameter (mm)	Designed pressure (MPa)	Designed wall temperature (°C)	Wall thickness (mm)	Material	Weight (ton)
3200	15.5	200	150	18MnMoNbR	286

Fig. 3. Ammonia synthesis reactor, 300,000 tons NH$_3$/year

The reactor for ammonia synthesis, 300,000 tons NH$_3$/year, employed the modified double cone sealing gasket, developed by the General Machinery Research Institute. This type of sealing gasket had many advantages, such as requiring smaller pre-seating force, whilst giving better self-tightening behavior and more reliable sealing effect. The Octagon gasket type sealing used in some of the imported 300,000 tons NH$_3$/year reactors always had trouble with serious leaking in operation. The leakage problem was not solved until the use of the modified double cone gasket (Lu and Xu, 1980). In order to form a complete series with the 300,000 tons NH$_3$/year plants, China fabricated her own urea plants capable of producing 240,000 and 520,000 tons urea/year. It is essential that all equipment used in urea plants should show high anti-corrosive behaviors. This problem is now successfully solved in China after a long period of 20 years to carry out research on this subject. In 1983, the first Chinese-produced urea reactor for 520,000 tons urea/year plants was turn out by the Nanjing Chemical Machinery Works. They used the multilayer construction; the inner core was made of stainless steel plates, which could withstand the corrosive medium. The inner surfaces of top and bottom heads were overlayed with stainless steel. Table 4 shows the technical parameters of this urea reactor, and Figure 4 shows its outward appearance during transportation (Yang, 1984).

TABLE 4   Technical Parameters of the Urea Reactor for
a 520,000 Tons urea/year Plant

Inside diameter (mm)	Designed pressure (MPa)	Designed wall temperature (°C)	Wall thickness (mm)	Length (M)	Weight (ton)
2800	16	198	124	36	322

Fig. 4. Urea reactor for a 520,000 tons urea/year plant

To satisfy the development of petroleum industry in China in the extension
of the processing of crude oils, the Lanzhou Petroleum and Chemical Machinery Works in 1965 for the first time fabricated a hydrogenation reactor of
the solid wall, rolled plate welded construction, the allowable wall
temperature being a maximum of 300°C. In 1974, they turned out another
reactor of the same construction, but the wall temperature was allowed to
reach 450°C. The technical parameters of the two reactors are shown in
Table 5.

TABLE 5   Technical Parameters of Hydrogenation Reactors
of Solid-wall, Rolled plate Welded Construction

No.	Inside diameter (mm)	Designed pressure (MPa)	Designed wall temperature (°C)	Wall thickness (mm)	Length of reactor (M)	Material
1	1800	15	300	88	18	20CrMo9*
2	2000	8	450	95	12	2¼Cr1Mo

* NOTE   20CrMo9 is a Chromium-molybdenum alloyed steel produced in the
Federal Republic of Germany

There were demands for hydrogenation reactors of larger capacities and
higher pressure in China in the early eighties, and research work was
carried out on this subject to employ the forging-welding construction by
the First Heavy Machinery Works. They completed the fabrication of 2
reactors, both of the forging-welding construction, in 1988. The technical
parameters of which are shown in Table 6.

1731

TABLE 6 Technical Parameters of Hydrogenation Reactors of Forging-welding Construction

No.	Inside diameter (mm)	Designed pressure (MPa)	Designed wall temperature (°C)	Wall thickness (mm)	weight (ton)	Material
1	1800	21	450	150	220	2¼Cr1Mo
2	3500	21	450	231	185	2¼Cr1Mo

The forgings of these two reactors were produced by the First Heavy Machinery Works, using material which showed low susceptibility to temper embrittlement. Its J factor $(Si+Mn)(P+Sn) \times 10^4 \leq 150\%$ and X factor $(10P +5Sb + 4Sn + As)/100 \leq 25$ ppm. Figure 5 shows the reactor I.D. 3,500 mm, during fabrication.

The reactors for nuclear power so far developed in China are of the PWR type. Pressure vessels for nuclear reactor were first fabricated in the late sixties for submarine use (Li and others, 1987). Figure 6 shows the overlay of stainless steel on the inside surface of a reactor vessel. Figure 7 shows the same reactor vessel under hydrostatic test.

A PWR power station of 300 MW capacity is now in the course of construction, the steam generator and pressure stabilizer of which were fabricated by the Shanghai Boiler Works. The pressure vessel needed for a PWR power station of 600 MW capacity will be fabricated in China.

Fig. 5. The hydrogenation reactor, I.D. 3,500mm, in the course of construction

Fig. 6. The overlay of stainless steel on the
inside surface of a reactor vessel

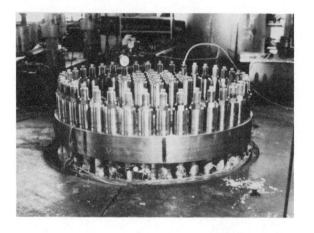

Fig. 7. A reactor vessel under hydrostatic test

PRESSURE VESSELS FOR SPECIAL PURPOSES

To cope with the production of new materials and to extend field of application of pressure vessels, there was a great development in China in the
field of special pressure vessels.

In 1963, to satisfy the urgent demands of equipment for the production of
high-pressure polyethylene, the General Machinery Research Institute made a
25-litre polyethylene reactor for laboratory research. In 1972, the Lanzhou
Petroleum & Chemical Machinery Works also made a similar reactor of 250-
litre capacity. Table 7 shows their relevent technical parameters.

TABLE 7   Technical Parameters of Polyethylene Reactors

Capacity (1)	Designed pressure (MPa)	Designed temperature (^{o}C)	Inside diameter (mm)	Material
25	150	200	150	34CrNi3MoA
250	195	285	305	34CrNi3MoA

Since the seventies, China has developed her own technology of isostatic treatment processes, of high pressure metal working processes and has carried out research in the field of geophysics. Vessels of superhigh pressure were in great need, and therefore were fabricated. Most of them were large, and vessel structures were mainly of the cylindrical multishell strink-fit construction and of the wire-wound construction. Table 8 shows the technical parameters of the superhigh pressure vessels used for the 6,000-ton and 15,000-ton isostatic presses manufactured by the Shanghai Heavy Machinery Works.

TABLE 8   Superhigh Pressure Vessels Used for the Isostatic
Presses, Technical Parameters

Total load of the isostatic press (ton)	Inside diameter (mm)	Outside diameter (mm)	Working pressure (MPa)	Construction
6,000	500	980	300	Shrink-fit
15,000	800	1334	300	Wire-wound

The steel wire used for the wire-wound vessel had a cross section of 4 x 1mm, the 0.2% proof stress, $\sigma_{0.2}$, of which $\geqslant$ 1,500 MPa. Figures 8 and 9 show the constructions of these two vessels of superhigh pressure, respectively.

A high temperature, superhigh pressure vessel was manufactured by the Shanghai Heavy Machinery Works in 1987 for the 800-ton Rock Rheology Testing Servo-Press which was needed in some of the researches carried out in the field of geophysics. The structure employed for the vessel was of three-layer shrink-fit construction. The relevant technical parameters are as follows:

Working pressure,   800 MPa
Working temperature,   400°C
Inside diameter,   100mm
Material used, Forgings of PCrNi3MoV

1734

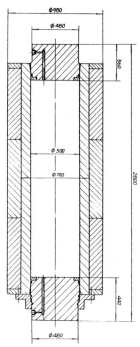

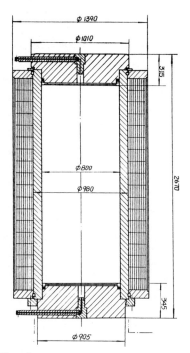

Fig. 8. Superhigh pressure vessel   Fig. 9. Superhigh pressure vessel
         of shrink-fit construction   of wire-wound construction

The mechanical properties of the forgings: yield strength, $\geq$ 1,120 MPa tensile strength, $\geq$ 1,200 MPa and elongation, $\geq$ 10%. Figure 10 shows the
outward appearance of the apparatus.

China possesses ample resources of titanium minerals. Therefore titanium is
being widely used in making pressure vessels and pressuried components for
some corrosive environments. For example, the carbon dioxide stripper of a
China's 240,000 tons urea/year plant was made of titanium to withstand the
corrosive conditions under high temperature and pressure. In view of the
extremely corrosive nature of the working medium in the urea plants it is
a common practice to use 00Cr25Ni22Mo2N stainless steel as the corrosion-
resistant material. In 1976 the Harbin Boiler Works fabricated its first
titanium CO_2 stripper in China. This stripper, after a long period of usage,
proved that titanium possesses even better corrosion-resistant properties
than 00Cr25Ni22Mo2N stainless steel (Bao and others, 1987). Furthermore, as
titanium has good resistance to damage by water containing chloride ions,
it is also used in making the condensers of steam turbines in plants near
the sea-coast in China. This has resulted in economics (Xu, 1986).

In her development of marine engineering, China made armour type diving
dress from titanium, which was said to be more functional than were the imported ones made of aluminum in that it can be satisfactorily used under a
300 M depth. Figure 11 shows one of the diving dresses made of titanium.

Fig. 10.   800-Ton Rock Rheology Testing Servo-Press

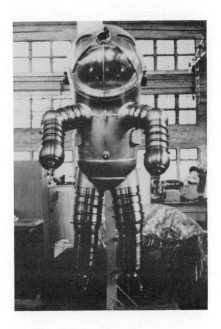

Fig. 11.   Titanium diving dress

STEEL USED BY THE PRESSURE VESSEL FABRICATORS

Most of the pressure vessels are made of steel. In order to meet the rapid growth of China's pressure vessel industry, it is necessary for her to develop continuously her steel grades or species for making pressure vessels with improved qualities. At the birth of the People's Republic of China in 1949, her metallurgical capacity was very limited, and steel plates were imported from other countries. However, during the past thirty odd years, China has developed many grades of pressure vessel steels by herself.

In the early fifties, mild steel such as G3 (A3), 20g etc. were used in making pressure vessels. In 1958, when first multilayer high pressure vessel was fabricated, 16Mn, a C–Mn steel, with a yield strength of 350 MPa, was employed. In 1964, 15MnTi with a yield strength of 400 MPa was used.

During the seventies many series of pressure vessel steels have been established, two of which are shown in Tables 9 and 10 – one for low-alloyed high strength steel series and the other for low-alloyed low temperature steel series.

TABLE 9 Low-alloyed High Strength Steel Series

Yield strength (MPa)	350	400	450	500	700
Steel grade	16Mn	15MnTi 15Mnv	15MnVN	14MnMoV 18MnMoNb 14MnMoVBXt	14MnMoNbB

TABLE 10 Low-alloyed Low Temperature Steel Series

Temperature range(°C)	–40	–41～–70	–71～–100
Steel grade	16Mn	09Mn2V 09 MnTiCuXt	06AlNbCuN 06MnNb

Recently, crack free steels of a yield strength of 500 MPa have also been developed for fabricating spherical vessels. Since 1980, following the rapid expansion of China's metallurgical industry, there has been great improvement in the properties of pressure vessel steels, especially the toughness. Till then, impact test specimens of U–notch, sampled in the lateral direction, were used to test the toughness of steel plates. Now, according to the national standards of testing toughness of the steel plates, it is specified to use the V–notch impact test specimens, also sampled in the lateral direction. The specifications of impact energy of steel plates of different grades at atmospheric temperature as listed in the catalogue of high quality steels by the Ministry of Metallurgy, have also been raised. For example, the impact energy of standard test specimen has been raised from 27J to 34J for 16Mn and 15MnVR, and from 34J to 41J for 15MnVNR and 18MnMoNbR. In normalized conditions better toughness for 16Mn and 15MnVR will result from treating by the ladle powder-injection process. Table 11 shows the test data.

TABLE 11   Toughness of 16Mn and 15MnV Steel Plates
in Normalized Condition

Steel grade	Thickness (mm)	A_{kv} (J)			
		20°C		−40°C	
		Longitudinal	Lateral	Longitudinal	Lateral
16Mn	32	180	157	130	110
15MnV	30	177	168	113	95

As for stainless steels, China is now producing many grade of stainless steel plates for the fabrication of pressure vessels used in corrosive enviroments. For making pressure vessels used in urea plants, China has also developed a type of Cr–Mn–N stainless steel.

For fabricating large sized pressure vessels of the forging-welding type, China has employed vacuum refining furnace (VRF) and mold steel degassing process (MSD) to produce forgings of better quality. The Shanghai Heavy Machinery Works has developed the electroslag remelting process (ESR) in the production of 205-ton steel ingot in their electroslag remelting furnace, from which a 150-ton forging can be made. The hydrogen content of the ingot is typically less than 2 ppm. Such forgings are used for the fabrication of reactor vessels.

CODES AND STANDARDS FOR PRESSURE VESSELS

Parallel with the development of pressure vessels in China, attention has also been given to the compilation of codes and standards for pressure vessels in order to insure the safe use of pressure vessels. The first pressure vessel standard ever compiled in China was known as "The Norm for the Design, Manufacturing and Inspection of Multilayer High-Pressure Vessels", which was jointly issued in 1959 by the First Ministry of Machine Building, Ministry of Chemical Industry, Ministry of Petroleum Industry and Ministry of Labor. This Norm was compiled with the purposes of satisfying the demand of the fabrication of multilayer high pressure vessels at that time. The second standard, known as "The Standard for Parts and Components of Chemical and Petroleum Refining Equipments" was jointly issued by the First Ministry of Machine Building, Ministry of Chemical Industry and Ministry of Petroleum Industry in 1960. It was compiled for the design of medium- and low-pressure vessels. The above two standards covered quite a wide range of pressure vessels and have been followed by nearly all the designing sectors for many years. In the later years of the 1960 decade and in those of the early seventies, for controlling the quality of pressure vessels and for updating manufacturing techniques, the First Ministry of Machine Building issued a series of "Specifications" for the fabrication and inspection of pressure vessels. The Ministry of Metallurgy also issued several professional standards for pressure vessel steels.

The scope of application for pressure vessels is growing rapidly. Strict requirements are imposed upon pressure vessels by the rapid growth of other industries. In 1977, the First Ministry of Machine Building, Ministry of Chemical Industry and Ministry of Petroleum Industry again jointly issued a new code known as "Regulations for the Design of Steel Pressure Vessels for Use in Petroleum and Chemical Industry: 1977" to update design method and rules to cover the whole range of pressure vessels from vacuum to high pressure. Based on the experience accumulated in the five years since 1977, new versions of the code were completed in 1982 and 1985 respectively. "Computer Programmes for Pressure Vessel Design" has also been recommended.

At this time, the general opinion seemed to favor the setting up of a National Standard for the design and manufacture of pressure vessels. Therefore in 1984 the National Bureau of Standards of the State Council of China decided to establish the China National Standards Committee of Pressure Vessels (CNSCPV), which was founded in July 1984. This committee is under the coordinative leadship of the National Bureau of Standards, China Petro-Chemical Corporation, Ministry of Chemical Industry, Ministry of Machine Building and Ministry of Labor and Personnel, and is authorized to undertake the formulation, revision, examination, interpretation, etc. of all the standards and specifications for the design, fabrication, inspection and acceptance of pressure vessels. The CNSCPV has set up a long-term program. The following National Standards, called GB in Chinese, of some pressurized components will be issued before the end of 1988 for the first time:

1. Welded Steel Pressure Vessels
2. Tube-and-Shell Heat Exchangers
3. Spherical Tanks

In addition, the following professional standards, called ZB in Chinese, will also be issued:

1. Welded Steel Pressure Vessels-- Alternative Standard
   (Pressure vessel codes based on stress analysis)
2. Standing Order for Pressure Vessel Steels
3. Non-destructive Examination for Pressure Vessels

Since 1950, the safety inspection of boilers and pressure vessels has been under the supervision of the Ministry of Labor. In order to strengthen the safety inspection of boilers and pressure vessels, the State Council issued a "Tentative Provision for Safety Inspection of Boilers and Pressure Vessels" in 1982 as a governmental document. According to this document, designers and manufacturers of boilers and pressure vessels must get permission for the design and fabrication of a certain class of pressure vessels. Following a little later, the Ministry of Labor and Personnel has set up the "Bureau of Boilers and Pressure Vessel Safety Supervision" as a responsible authority for the execution of the "Tentative Provisions" including the certification work.

Rules for the assessment of defects are urgently needed for both in-process inspection and in-service inspection. Research on fracture mechanics in China has been carried out on a large scale since 1971. It is reported that, application of fracture mechanics to the safety evaluation of high pressure vessels, spherical pressure vessels and boiler drums with cracks in the welds have been successful. The working group organized by the General Machinery Research Institute (under the Ministry of Machine Building) and the Chemical Machinery Research Institute (under the Ministry of Chemical Industry), after carrying out research on pressure vessels with cracks for several years, published a guidance document known as "Rules for the Assessment of Defects in Pressure Vessels". In the document, both the stress intensity factor method and the COD method are adopted, for the assessment of defects in pressure vessels.

In the near future, the CNSCPV will undertake the Compilation of the Professional Standards known as "Defect Assessment for In-service Pressure Vessels", including assessment ranges, requirements, criteria, fracture mechanics formulation, failure diagrams, residual life prediction etc.

In order to keep up with international standards in the manufacturing, some machinery works in China are applying for certificates from well-known organizations in the West, such as ASME, API etc. In 1984, for the first time, the Lanzhou Petroleum and Chemical Machinery Works obtained permission, from ASME to use the ASME Stamps U and U2 for some of their products. Thereafter, several pressure vessel fabricators in China have been granted the Certificates to use the ASME Stamps U and U2 too.

EPILOGUE

During the past forty years, there has also been remarkable progress in the field of education and scientific researches concerning pressure vessels in the People's Republic of China. In 1952, our universities started to train engineers and researchers devoting themselves to the progress of pressure vessel technology. At the present time, many universities do this, ten of them admit post-graduate students pursuing master degrees, but only three of them confer Ph.D degrees. The General Machinery Research Institute was established in 1956 by the former First Ministry of Machine Building. One of main activities of this institute is to carry out researches on topics relevant to pressure vessel technology. Thereafter, many industrial departments and universities also establised research institutes, one after another, to carry out researches concerning the design, materials, fracture and fatigue as well as fabrication and inspection of pressure vessels.

In 1980, the Chinese Pressure Vessel Institution (CPVI) was founded as one of the secondary organizations of the Chinese Mechanical Engineering Society (CMES), which was founded in 1952. The CPVI organizes the pressure vessel technologists in China to participate in those technical conferences exchanging informations and views, issues the bimonthly journal "Pressure Vessel Technology", and also establishes connections with the technical

1740

societies of pressure vessel technologists of other countries. The progress made in education and scientific researches in the field of pressure vessel technology is enhancing the progress of pressure vessel production in China.

With the development of national economy in China there are necessities to set up more modern plants of chemical fertilizers, petroleum refining, petro-chemical products, nuclear power and other new branches of industries. In China, the pressure vessel technologists are being confronted with vessels of even more severe specifications and even bigger capacities. It is our view that the international exchanges of technical views and cooperations on topics of mutual interests must be strengthened in order to solve the many of the problems which we are facing and to enhance the progress of pressure vessel technology in China.

REFERENCES

Bao, Hong-Shu and others (1987). The History of Development of Chinese petroleum, Chemical and General Machine Building Industry (in Chinese). China Machinery Press, Beijing, China
Li, Jiao and others (1987). Chinese Nuclear Industry at the present time (In Chinese). China Social Sciences Press, Beijing, China
Liu, Cengdian (1959). Journal of Heavy and General Machinery, 12, 31-33. (In Chinese)
Lu, Li-Rong and Wen-Hua Xu (1980). Journal of Chemical and General Machinery 9, 45-53. (In Chinese)
Xu, Xiang-Yin (1986). pressure Vessel Technology, 2, 76-79. (In Chinese)
Yang, Qin-Sheng (1984). Pressure Vessel Technology, 4, 66-69. (In Chinese)

PANEL ON SEISMIC DESIGN OF PRESSURE VESSELS AND PIPING

INTRODUCTION TO THE PANEL SESSION
"Seismic Design of Pressure Vessels and Piping"

H. Akiyama

University of Tokyo, Tokyo, Japan

Zhexian Wang

Lanshou Petrochemical Design Institute of China
Petrochemical Corp., Xigu, Lanzhou, Gansu, China

The aim of this session is to make clear the essential matters
concerning seismic design in the field of pressure vessels and
pipings. Compared to other loads such as gravity and operation
loads, seismic loads have a high complexity and uncertainty.
On the other hand, an earthquake is a phenomenon which occurs
within a limited short time, and the energy input to a structure
exerted by an earthquake becomes a finite amount. Therefore,
the behavior of a structure can be traced by the following
equilibrium of energy during the earthquake.

$$W_e + W_h + W_p = E,$$

where W_e:the elastic vibrational energy in astructure,
W_h:the energy absorption due to miscellaneous
damping effects,
W_p:the cumulative inelastic strain energy developed
by a structure,
E :the total energy input exerted by an earthquake.

Inherently, steel structures are equipped with an abundant
capacity for energy absorption and the main source of this
capacity is ascribed to W_p. Since E is a rather stable quantity,
less influenced by structural characteristics, W_e can be
remarkably reduced, provided that a structure can fully develop
its energy absorption capacity.
The typical collapse modes of vessels and pipings are the
fracture of their components and the overturning of the whole
structure. Buckling is enumerated as one of collapse mode in the
case of gravity loading. The reduction of the vertical loading
capacity ensuing the occurrence of buckling leads a structure to
collapse under gravity loading. The situation for earthquakes,
however, differs in the fact that the reduction of horizontal
loading capacity does not immediately mean the collapse of the
structure, as far as the energy absorption capacity is not
exhausted. Nevertheless, buckling can be another important
phenomenon to be considered for structures subjected to
earthquakes, since buckling promotes large amplitude strains
and excessive deformations which may cause a low cycle fatigue
type of fracture and the overturning of the structure due to

the loss of vertical equilibrium.
There are two kind of approaches to analyze the behavior of
structures under earthquakes. One is linear analysis in which
the nonlinear behavior of structures is approximated by a linear
behavior incorporated with equivalent damping values. This
approach can be successfully applied to complicated systems like
piping systems. This approach, however, may lose its applicability
for highly nonlinear structures in which strain concentration at
localized points is very likely to occur.
Another approach is direct nonlinear analysis. On the basis of
an adequate hyateresis rule(restoring force characteristics),
the realistic response of a structure can be estimated by this
approach. However, because of a multitude of parameters involved
in this approach, nonlinear analysis has some difficulties as a
general method. In this context, together with a rigorous
approach, some simplified methods are strongly needed which are
easy to apply and lead to satisfying results.

Main topics selected are as follows.

1. Earthquake resistant design for piping systems
   1.1 Recent advances in evaluation of damping in nuclear piping
       systems
       by Dr T.H. Liu, Westinghouse Electric Corp., U.S.A.
   1.2 Evaluation of ultimate strength
       by Dr J. D. Wörner, König & Heunish, FR Germany

2. Earthquake resistant design for vessels influenced by buckling
   2.1 Upon the design of structures in case of seismic buckling
       by Dr A. Combescure, Centre D'Etudes Nucleaires de Saclay,
       DEMT, France
   2.2 Recent studies on shear buckling of cylindrical shells
       due to seismic loads
       by Dr S. Matsuura, Central Research Institute of Electric
       Power Industry, Japan
   2.3 Evaluation of buckling and collapse of cylindrical vessel
       due to earthquake loadings
       by Dr T. Yuhara, Mitsubishi Heavy Industries, Japan

Dr Liu presents the state of the art in the U.S.A. concerning
damping values applied to the linear analysis of piping systems.
Dr Wörner discusses rigorous nonlinear analysis and proposes an
alternative simplified method termed "ultimate strength method".
Dr Combescure provides some basic insight in the design of
structures against seismic buckling. The sensitivity of buckling
load to the initial imperfection under seismic excitations is
discussed in comparison to the case of static gravity loads.
It is also pointed out that the effect of dynamic loading on
buckling loads cannot be dismissed under a certain condition
associated with frequencies of vessels.
Dr Matsuura presents the state of the art in Japan concerning
experimental research on cylindrical shells subjected to seismic
loads. Recent data covers not only buckling loads but also
post-buckling behavior.
Dr Yuhara discusses the design concept for buckling-prone
cylindrical vessels, making allowance for energy absorption in
the post-buckling range.

RECENT ADVANCES IN EVALUATION OF DAMPING IN NUCLEAR PIPING SYSTEMS

T. H. Liu

General Technology System Division
Westinghouse Electric Corporation, U.S.A.

SUMMARY

For the last twenty years the structural damping has become one of the most
discussed issues in the dynamic analysis of nuclear piping systems. This
parameter provides great influence to the design of piping systems through
dynamic response analysis, where the magnitude of piping system responses
depend on the magnitude of damping. The actual damping of piping system in
a nuclear power plant is physically complex. To dynamically analyze the piping system with modern technology requires simplification of structural damping. One way in simplification is to define a unique damping value for the
complete piping system, regardless of such variables: (i) magnitude of the
input motion, (ii) pipe sizes, (iii) support types and conditions, (iv) internal pressure and, (v) pipe insulations. For the design purposes in the
piping industry where conservatism is most valued such simplification is
technically acceptable with a great deal of saving in calculation. Therefore,
in the early 1970s, (1973), the United States Atomic Energy Commission (USAEC)
had adopted and issued a set of simplified damping values, Regulatory Guide
(RG) 1.61, for the use in seismic analysis. The American Society of Mechanical
Engineers Boiler and Pressure Vessel Code (ASME Code) had quickly endorsed
the RG 1.61 for the use in piping industry.

The recommended damping values in RG 1.61 for seismic analysis were based on
the gathered best available experimental data and on the opinions of the
leading experts in the field. The main objective was to establish a set of
damping values that could easily be used by the analyst and that would be
conservative for deriving seismic loads in the piping design. It is the so
called "conservatively" design concept in seismic that lead to the over-prediction in seismic responses of displacement and stresses. As a result of
such over-prediction, unnecessary seismic supports are added to ensure the
system responses are under the code allowables and to maintain a large design
margin for seismic loads.

In the early 1980s, problems associated with conservative seismic design
margins by using conservative damping values had been recognized. It was
widely believed that the penalty of an overly conservative designed piping
system for seismic loads is the excessive restriction on thermal motion
during the plant operation. Such restriction has resulted in piping systems

less able to respond freely at operating condition, thereby make them poten-
tially more susceptible to thermal cracking. In remeding this problem, the
Pressure Vessel Research Committee (PVRC) of the Welding Research Council
had revisited the existing test data plus the more recent experimental results
in damping and arrived at a set of more realistic damping values rather than
the conservative values provided in RG 1.61. The PVRC has recently recommended
a simple damping curve which is frequency dependent and applicable for both
OBE and SSE earthquakes.

The PVRC damping has been adopted on a case-by-case basis by the USNRC and has
been approved for inclusion in the ASME Code as Code Case N-411. This simplified damping curve does provide some relief in terms of taking out extra
conservation. As a result, many unwanted and sometimes unreliable seismic
supports such as snubbers can be removed from the plant. This provides a
great improvement in the plant cost associated with design/analysis and in-
spection/maintenance.

Recognizing the complexity and variations in the damping of piping systems,
research in U.S. had moved further since the publication of PVRC damping.
Currently, there are being three major programs carried out by the EPRI and
INEL. In one of the two EPRI programs, parameters which are the Principal
factors influencing damping are studied using engineering tools. The input
excitation parameters, physical design parameters and system response parameters are included in the study. In the other EPRI program, which has the
objective of evaluating the alternative design rules for piping systems,
piping components and systems are tested at high amplitudes and low frequencies. In the third program with INEL, the effort is to establish best-estimate
damping values for use in the dynamic analysis of piping systems. Statistical
evaluation of PWR piping damping for the PRA analysis is being conducted using
collected data from their piping damping data bank. A more detailed report on
some of the results from the afore-mentioned programs will be prepared in the
final write-up.

EVALUATION OF ULTIMATE STRENGTH

J.D. Wörner*

*König und Heunisch, Beratende Ingenieure, Frankfurt/M., FRG

ABSTRACT

For the determination of the ultimate loading capacity of single degree of freedom systems approximate and rigorous methods are available which take into account different types of nonlinear effects. The results of such an estimation can be drawn in form of nonlinear response spectra.

As far as multi degree of freedom systems are concerned more efforts have to be done in order to consider the stress redistribution caused by a local effect. Examples show the large influence of the stress redistribution to the overall response. A method was elaborated which allows to estimate the nonlinear response taking into account various local effects such as gap, sliding and yielding. This method is based on progressive modifications of the system according to the local effect. The nonlinear calculation is limited to modal nonlinear single degree of freedom systems.

KEYWORDS

Ultimate strength, local effects, gap, friction, yielding, stress redistribution, approximate nonlinear method

INTRODUCTION

In the past various attempts were made to determine the ultimate strength of systems under seismic loading. In these investigations one has to consider all important effects for instance local sliding, gaps and yielding. Many researchers (Newmark (1970), Housner (1956)) tried to define approximate methods which allow an engineer to estimate the nonlinear response of a system without doing expensive large computer calculations. These investigations were more or less limited to single-degree of freedom systems and certain effects, namely yielding. During the last years the capability of computers increased rapidly and it is no longer a problem to calculate the nonlinear seismic response of systems taking into account all possible effects. But although these computational capabilities are available, there is still a need for approximate methods in order to study the influence of local effects, to get a quick understanding of the contributing factors and to optimize a system.

This paper will show at first some results for single degree of freedom systems and then one method will be described which allows an engineer to determine approximately the nonlinear response of a multi-degree-of-freedom system.

Because all the investigations reported herein are focussed on the behaviour of equipments, vessels and piping a typical floor response is chosen as input motion (Fig. 1).

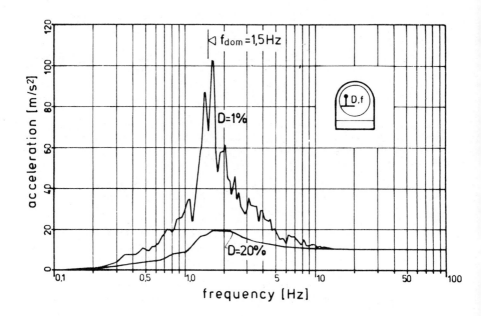

SINGLE DEGREE OF FREEDOM SYSTEMS

As it was stated above there are a lot of reports about the seismic response of single degree of freedom systems (Newmark (1970), Housner (1956), Akiyama (1985), König (1985)) with local nonlinearities under seismic excitation. Approximate and rigorous methods are easily available. Fig. 2 shows results of a computer program which automatically determines the nonlinear response spectra for yielding, gap and sliding.

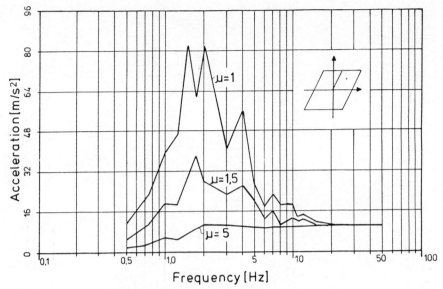

Fig. 2 Nonlinear response spectra, yielding

Such results give the engineer an understanding of into the influence of a
local effect in the whole frequency range. Thus possible misinterpretation
of results of a single nonlinear calculation can be avoided effectively.

MULTI DEGREE OF FREEDOM SYSTEMS

As far as multi degree of freedom systems are concerned much more efforts
have to be done to determine the ultimate dynamic strength. Rigorous methods
are meanwhile available but show some disadvantages such as:

o lack of information about the influence of single local effects,
o lack of information about the influence of uncertainty of the input

One important aspect of the behaviour of MDOF-systems is the stress redistribution due to a local effect.
To show the influence of stress redistribution the maximum relative displacement of a two degree of freedom system with yielding under seismic
excitation are drawn in Fig. 3 for changing yield limits of the outer
springs.

1750

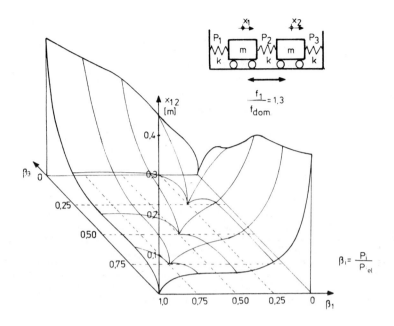

Fig. 3 Rel. displacement between mass 1 and mass 2

This extreme example points out the necessity to consider the stress redistribution in the analysis.

Based on this conclusion, the static plastic analysis and the modal analysis an approximate method has been developed which consists of the following main points:

a) determination of the eigenfrequencies and mode shapes of the given system
b) determination of modal stresses for an unit acceleration
c) determination of local effects and respective modal acceleration level
d) modification of the system according to the local effect
e) a), b) for the changed system
f) repeat d), e) until ultimate strength is reached
g) formulation of modal nonlinear single degree of freedom systems
h) calculation of the modal response
i) calculation of the overall response.

Compared to the normal modal analysis only the formulation of the modal nonlinear single degree of freedom systems is a really new step. All other steps are basically the same as in ordinary calculations. Fig. 4 shows some local effects and the respective modifications of the system.

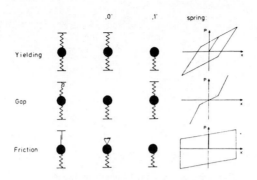

Fig. 4 Local effects and respective modifications

From comparative studies the method could be verified (Wörner (1986)). Here an example using a shaking table experiment with a piping is given. Fig. 5 shows the considered system. After step c) it was stated that the piping will yield at certain points. The effect of the yielding was considered by weakening of the piping according to the moment curvature relation.

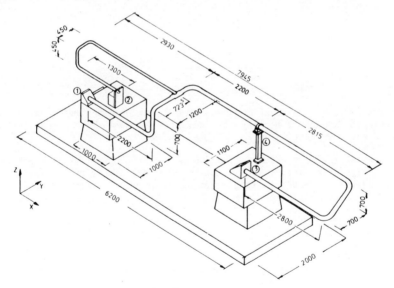

Fig. 5 Example – piping

The resulting modal nonlinear springs are given in Fig. 6. With these springs a nonlinear calculation was performed. The response quantities which were got are shown in table 1 together with the measured values. A very good agreement could be stated.

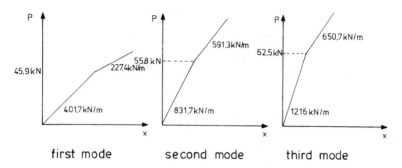

first mode   second mode   third mode

Fig. 6   Modal nonlinear springs

TABLE 1   Response quantities

		appr. Method	Experiment
③	ε_1	4,0‰	3,8‰
	ε_2	3,0‰	2,5‰
①	ε_1	0,75‰	0,8‰
	ε_2	0,70‰	0,75‰
②	ε_1	3,4‰	2,6‰
	ε_2	1,4‰	2,0‰

CONCLUSION

As far as single degree of freedom systems are concerned nonlinear response spectra are favourable because they give an overview of the response in the whole frequency range.

For multi degree of freedom systems it is not enough to take into account of local energy dissipation, but one has to consider stress redistribution. The approximation presented in this paper is based on well known methods and is able to consider different types of local effects.

REFERENCES

Newmark, N.M. (1970). Current trends in the Seismic Analysis and Design of High Rise Structures. Earthquake Engineering, Prentice Hall Inc., Englewood Cliffs.
Housner, G.W. (1956). Limit Design of Structures to resist Earthquakes. WCEE, Berkeley.
Akiyama, H. (1985). Earthquake-Resistant Limit-State Design for Buildings. University of Tokyo Press.
König, G., J.D. Wörner (1985). Nonlinear effects in Component-Structure-Interaction and their Influence on the Dynamic Behaviour of the Components, 8th SMIRT   K 9/8
Wörner, J.D. (1986). Estimation of the Behaviour of Structures with localized Nonlinearities using an Ultimate State method. Nuclear Engineering and Design   96, 441-446.

UPON THE DESIGN OF STRUCTURES IN CASE OF SEISMIC BUCKLING

A. COMBESCURE

(C.E.A. - CEN/SACLAY -DEMT/SMTS/LAMS - 91191 GIF SUR YVETTE (FRANCE))

ABSTRACT

The aim of the paper is to give some insight in the design of structures against seismic buckling. In the first part the classical "static" aproach is presented and discussed.

In the second part the effect of dynamic loading is introduced.

In the last part of the paper a design methodology is presented which takes into account the frequency characteristics of the seismic loads.

KEY WORDS

Buckling ; seismic imperfection ; dynamic design ; finite element ; CASTEM system.

1. THE CLASSICAL STATIC PROCEDURE TO PREVENT DYNAMIC BUCKLING

In this part we are going to describe the classical way to design a structure against dynamic buckling. We shall, on purpose, omit all safety coefficient throughout this paper. We shall then discuss a little bit this classical procedure and finally we shall also give an application to a typical structure. On this structure we shall try to give an explanation of some paradox that can be observed.

1.1 THE CLASSICAL STATIC METHOD

The method consists essentially to design the structure loaded by a dynamic loading as if it were loaded by a static loading. Let us suppose that the structure is loaded by a load having the equation :

(1) $f(x,y,z) * \sin (\Omega * t)$

where $f(x,y,z)$ is the spatial shape of the load, and omega the pulsation of the load, and t the time. The method consists simply to look for the static buckling of the structure under the loading $f(x,y,z)$. If the critical load factor is less then 1 we shall predict dynamic buckling otherwise we shall predict no ruin. We must first make one important remark : we cannot, in the general case, make the hypothesis that the loading is described by the separated equation (1). In general there is a spatial loading which is not in phase between all points. We than have the problem of defining the correct load.

1.2 CHOICE OF THE GOOD SPATIAL SHAPE OF THE LOAD

There are at least two ways to proceed. The first one consists of a standard mode superposition method, taking into account the input spectrum and damping on each eigen mode. This method is rather simple, but has the drawback to produce loads which have no sign, so that the worst combination of sign has to be chosen. But what is the "worst" combination ? The worst combination is the one that leads to the minimun safety factor on buckling : in some cases the choice of the signs is a rather simple game but in other cases the most critical situation is not an easy guess. The second method consists of making a certain number of direct step by step analysis with various damping factor (eg 1 % ; 1.2 % ; 1.4 %) : from this analysis it is possible to have the whole history of the loadings and to observe their variation with damping. In this case there is no problem of sign of the loading. We netherthless have to face here a huge number of results in which we shall have to choose the worst " instant" : here the problem is still more difficult than in the previous approach because of the number of possible critical "instants".

1.3 THE CRITERIA TO CHOOSE THE WORST LOADING

When we have to face elastic buckling the choice is rather simple .The worst loading is the one leading to the smallest load multiplier for buckling. When plasticity occurs in the buckling, material non linearity has also to be taken into account.

We could give the following procedure to define the critical load multiplier λ_c for a given shape of the loading :

1 - Compute the elastic buckling multiplier λ_e.
2 - Compute the load multiplier at which plasticity occurs λ_y.
3 - Let us call the Young's modulus E and the tengeant modulus H ; if λ_e less than λ_y the load multiplier λ_c is λ_e : if not, λ_c is the maximum between λ_y and λ_e * H/E. With this procedure the different dynamic shape of the loading can be compared. And a shape can be chosen to perform a fully nonlinear static analysis to predict the buckling. The way to proceed to have a reasonable accuracy in buckling predictions has been described in details in [2] and [10].

1.4 APPLICATION TO A TYPICAL CASE

On this example we hope to show the importance of the choice of the shape of the loading on the prediction of buckling.

1.4/1 Geometry material data loading boundary conditions

The structure studied is a cylinder whose nominal radius is .475m whose height is 2.0 m. The cylinder is clamped at its base. It is stiffened at its top. The material is a steel whose YOUNG'S modulus is 180.000 MPA with a conventional .2 % yield stress of 253 MPA. This cylinder is filled with water up to the level of 1.85 m from its base. It is put on an horizontal shaking table which produces a mode one pressure whose spatial shape can be observed on fig 1. (for more details on this pressure field and the comparison with experiments see reference [11])the maximum measured imperfection is of about 1 mm.

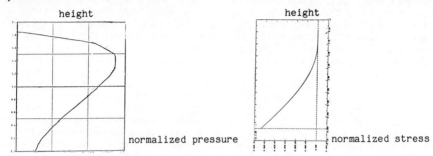

Figure 1 : Mode 1 : Pressure   Figure 2 : Mode 1 : Axial stress

1.4/2 Predictions on the perfect structure

With these data, the permanent hydrostatic pressure generates a permanent tensile hoop stress at the base of the cylinder, and the dynamic mode one pressure generates a shear and bending stress. The axial stress profile given on fig 2. The maximum is at the base. The prediction (by finite element analysis with INCA code of the CASTEM SYSTEM [1]) of the buckling modes lead to three types of buckling : an external pressure buckling for a dynamic pressure of .0160 MPA whose shape can be observed on fig 3 ; a shear buckling for a pressure of .03 MPA (see fig 4) ; and a bending buckling for a pressure of .02 MPA (see fig 5). The bending buckling pressure can be obtained directly by applying the KOITER's formula to the axial stress at the base of the cylinder. From this result we could conclude that the buckling that will occur shall be an external pressure type of buckling. Why is it not the observed experimental ruin ?

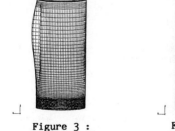  

Figure 3 :
Pressure buckling mode
0.015 MPA

Figure 4 :
Shear buckling
0.03 MPA

Figure 5 :
Bending buckling
0.02 MPA

1.4/3 Effect of the imperfections. The paradox

It is well known that these type of very thin cylinders are very sensitive to initial imperfections when they are loaded by an axial compression. If we would take the reduction of buckling load for a cylinder under uniform

axial compression according to KOITER, we should have a reduction of a
factor of more than three on the buckling load.
This would lead to a buckling pressure of 60 MPA which is much too low
compared with experimental recorded buckling pressure. Why is that not the
case here ? It that because of dynamic effects ? Is that because of an
other factor ? Let us now study the effect of imperfections on our cylinder
loaded by an axial compression due to a bending loading. In our case the
mode 1 loading can be replaced by an axisymmetric linearly varying stress.
This cylinder, considered as perfect, buckles for the same maximum axial
stress then the previous one. The buckling load of the imperfect structure
with a linearily varying stress profile is only 60 % of the buckling load
of the perfect structure. If we now take into account the true axial stress
profile we come to a still less sensitive structure to imperfections. The
ruin occurs at a load of about 70 % of that of the perfect structure with
combination of plasticity and of large displacements in the imperfect zone
(see fig. 6 for the final shape of the structure). We finally come to the
prediction that the structure shall fail with an axial compression failure.
This failure is caused by bending associated to mode 1 load at a pressure
of about .014 MPA. This pressure is lower than the buckling load associated
with external pressure wich is .015 MPA (taking into account the effect of
imperfection on this type of mode).

1.5 CONCLUSION

We have shown that the shape of loading is very important in the buckling
analysis. In our case the same initial imperfections reduces of a factor 3
the buckling load with a uniform axial load and the reduction is only 30 %
when the dynamic shape of the loading is applied.

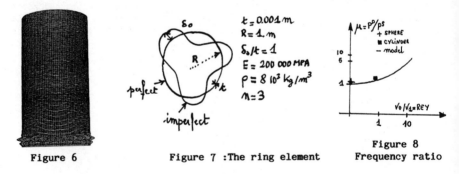

| Figure 6 | Figure 7 :The ring element | Figure 8 Frequency ratio |

2. THE DYNAMIC BUCKLING PROBLEM

Many experiments have been performed throught the world to study dynamic
buckling for instance (see ref. 3, 4, 8, 9). Let us now build a theoretical
model.

2.1 THE RING MODEL

Let us consider an annular ring with an imperfection δ_0 on a Fourier
mode n. This ring element can be represented by one COMU element of the
INCA program of the CASTEM SYSTEM [1], [6], [7]. The ring is supposed to
behave elastically the mass matrix being diagonal.

2.2 EFFECT OF THE RATE OF LOADING

A dynamic external pressure $P(t) = P_0 \sin \omega_0 t$ ($\omega_0 = 2\pi\nu_0$) is applied to the imperfect ring.
The load level P_0 is increased by steps of $P_E/10$, P_E being the elastic bifurcation load. Figure 7 defines very simply the data. The computations are done with the COMU element of the computer code INCA.
The structure is loaded with a periodic excitation which is either slow or fast or of the same speed than the frequency (ν_1) of the buckling mode (which is also the vibration mode).
We have chosen 3 cases :
      (a) $\nu_0/\nu_1 = 0.1$ - slow,
      (b) $\nu_0/\nu_1 = 1$ - medium
      (c) $\nu_0/\nu_1 = 10$ - fast
Let us call REY this ratio.

- For cases (a) and (c) the damping has very little effect and it is found that :
(a) if the structure is loaded slowly it buckles at a pressure $P(t)$ which is the Euler bifurcation load P_E.
(b) if the structure is loaded rapidly (case (c)) it can stand a dynamic pressure ($P(t)$) which is 5 times greater than the Euler bifurcation load without buckling.

- On case (b) the load level which can be supported depends on the damping factor. When taking a damping factor of 1 % we obtain a maximum standable dynamic load of 1.5 P_E.

If we plot on a diagram the different computed points we obtain the type of curve given on figure 8. The abscissa is the ratio REY. On the y-axis is the ratio between the dynamic buckling load and the static one.
On this curve it is obvious that a periodic pressure is less efficient if it is applied at a high frequency than if it applied at a low frequency.
The same concept is applied to the experimental result.

- For the C.E.A. spheres the two frequencies are :
$\nu_0 \simeq 30$ Hz, $\nu_1 = 1000$ Hz (computed)
The dynamic load is applied very slowly.

- For the C.E.A. cylinders the two frequencies are :
$\nu_0 = 27$ Hz, $\nu_1 = 27$ Hz.

From figure 8 we observe that the experimental buckling pressures are in good agreement with the predicted ones by the model given above.

3. PROPOSED METHODOLOGY

The methodology for a design against dynamic elastic buckling is the following :

(a) Compute the static buckling associated with the dynamic load (buckling load λ_B^S eigen mode u_B).
(b) From that determine the eigen frequency of this mode ν_1. If there is no fluid this eigen frequency is given by the equation :
$$\nu_1 = \frac{1}{2\Pi} \sqrt{\frac{u_B \, K \, u_B}{u_B \, M \, u_B}}$$
      (K : stiffness ; M : mass matrix)
(c) Calculate the ratio between the frequency of excitation ν_0 and ν_1 :
$$R = \frac{\nu_0}{\nu_1}$$

1758

(d) From figure 8 get the amplification factor μ.
(e) Calculate the dynamic buckling load λ_B^D by the formula
$$\lambda_B^D = \mu \; \lambda_B^S$$

A general simple methodology to design against dynamic elastic buckling of a structure has been given.
A wider qualification of the method has to be done especially on existing experimental data.

REFERENCES

[1] Combescure, A., Static and dynamic buckling of thin shells. Nuclear Eng. and Design (1986) n° 92 - pp. 339-354
[2] Recent advances in nuclear componant testing and theoretical studies on buckling A.S.M.E. - P.V.P. Vol. 89 San Antonio, Texas - 1984 (13 papers on the subject)
[3] Clough, P., and Niva, A., Experimental evaluation of seismic design method for broad cylindrical tank (BERKELEY - EERC 77/10) (BERKELEY - EERC 78/04)
[4] Shibata, H., Seismic capacity testing of a thin wall for 500 ton cylindrical tank (University of Japan) private communication
[5] Combescure, A., Modèle d'oscillation non linéaire à un degré de liberté RAPPORT DEMT 84/008
[6] Combescure, A., Equations d'équilibre et de flambement d'un anneau avec défaut RAPPORT DEMT 81/142
[7] Aita, S., Combescure, A. and Gibert, R.J., Imperfections on thin axisymetric shells fluid structure interaction aspects (1987) SMIRT 9 - Paper B5/1 - Lausanne
[8] Dostal and all, Benchmark study of shear buckling of a cylindrical vessel (1986) Nuclear Science and Technology - EUR 10592 EN CEC
[9] Guigiani, Vigni and all, Dynamic stability of fluid coupled cylinders : Expt. investigation (1987) SMIRT 9 - Vol. E pp. 287-293 - Lausanne
[10] RCC-MR - Appendix Z
[11] Combescure, A., Queval, J.C., Aillot, M., Dynamic behavior of liquid storage tank, SMIRT 9 (1987) Vol. K2, pp. 781-786.

RECENT STUDIES ON SHEAR BUCKLING OF CYLINDRICAL SHELLS
DUE TO SEISMIC LOADS

S. Matsuura

Earthquake Engineering and Structure Department, Abiko Research Laboratory
Central Research Institute of Electric Power Industry
1646 Abiko Abiko-shi Chiba-ken Japan

ABSTRACT

Vertical short cylindrical shells which are subjected to horizontal seismic loads can fail by buckling in shear. This paper is to intruduce the recent experimental and numerical studies on shear buckling of cylindrical shells. In particular, concentrating on main vessels of the fast breeder reactor, estimation methods of shear buckling strength are described.

KEY WORDS

Shear buckling; fast breeder reactor; cylindrical shell; elastic-plastic buckling

INTRODUCTION

Recent Studies in Japan

Japan is located in earthquake prone zone. For long years, therefore, the people has been showing keen interest in the destruction of structures due to seismic loads. As a result, many studies have been also made in relation to the buckling caused by seismic loads. Summarized in table 1 are the typical experimental studies relating mainly to tanks and cantileverd cylindrical shells.

Recent Studies in Foreign Countries

Shear buckling of cylindrical shells under seismic loads has been studied in foreign countries mainly concerning the steel containment vessel of nuclear reactor and the main vessel of fast breeder reactor. Recent studies are shown in table 2.

SHEAR BUCKLING OF CYLINDERS

Governing Parameters

Typical examples of the shear buckling mode and of the axial compression buckling mode are given in Figs. 1a and 1b. As clearly seen from the figures, shear buckling shows slant wrinkles while axial compression buckling shows diamond -shaped patterns. In the case of buckling under transverse shearing load, the maximum axial compression stress occurs due to bending moment at the lower end of the compressed side. Therefore, buckling may be caused by bending at the place. In this case, wrinkles similar to the axial compression buckling mode appear locally. On the shear side 90 degrees from the force-applied direction, on the other hand, shearing stresses prevail, resulting in the shear buckling.

Such a difference in buckling mode is significantly affected by shape parameters, radius-to-thickness ratio(R/t), length-to-radius ratio(L/R) and load applied height-to-radius ratio(H/R), etc. The H/R represents maximum bending stress to maximum shearing stress ratio. This is because load Q, which is loaded at height of H, will cause bending and shearing stress circumferential distributions as $(QH/\pi R^2 t)\cdot\cos\theta$ and $(Q/\pi Rt)\cdot\sin\theta$ at the lower end of the cylinder, respectively.(See Fig.2) In the case of large R/t, elastic buckling occurs and small R/t causes elastc-plastic or plastic buckling.

Fig.3 shows the example of experimental results (Akiyama,Yuhara,1985) concerning the changes in buckling mode under the various values of shape parameters.

Material Parameters

Whether material nonlinearity may act or not on the occurence of buckling depends on the elastic-plastic behaviors and shape parameters of the cylinder. In the case of short cylindrical shells made of stainless steel or mild steel, R/t of approximately 300 or more falls in the range of elastic buckling, while 100 and below is in the range of plastic buckling. And R/t of about 100 thru 300 falls in transient zone of elastic-plastic buckling.

Effects of Initial Imperfections

As for the buckling phenomena, initial imperfections in shape and in material characteristics have genarally great effect on buckling and on the load-displacement relations. This effect, for example, is very significant over the buckling of cylinders under axial compression. In the case of large R/t, it is experimentally observed that such imperfections decrease the axial compression buckling load about 20% against the theoretical one. Significant drop, therefore, has been taken into account in design codes and standards. The imperfections, however, are less influential over shear buckling. Besides, they tend to be less influential over the plastic buckling area than elastic one. Figs.4 and 5 show the examples of the numerical results of shape imperfection upon buckling loads. These results indicate discrepancies in the effects according to the difference in initial imperfection mode. In the case of severe imperfection mode which has eigenmode and initial maximum deflection equal to the plate thickness of a cylindrical shell, elastic-plastic buckling load decreases to approximately 80% of that without imperfecrions. This shows that shear buckling is less sensitive to initial imperfections than axial compression buckling.

Interactions of Bending and Shearing in Buckling under Transverse Shearing Loads

As far as the buckling under transverse shearing load in which shearing and bending load act simaltaneously, interaction may be caused between bending and shearing. In the case of cylinders having R/t of approximately 300 and below, plastisity may be also concerned as one of the factors. As far as interaction is concerned between bending and shearing, various relations may be assumed. It is considered, however, that buckling load quadratic interaction rule can be applied in the elastic buckling area.(Akiyama,Yuhara,Shimizu,Takahashi,1985)

$$(\sigma_{b,cr}/\sigma_{b\theta})^2 + (\tau_{cr}/\tau_s)^2 = 1 \qquad (1)$$

Where, $\sigma_{b\theta}$ is theoretical value of elastic buckling stress due to bending, τ_s is theoretical value of elastic buckling due to shearing, while $\sigma_{b,cr}$ and τ_{cr} represent the buckling stress of bending and shearing, respectively.

This quadratic interaction rule is equivalent to the following linear equation, in consideration of the distribution of bending and shearing stresses. (Yuhara,Tashimo,1987)

$$\sigma_b(\theta)/\sigma_{b\theta} + \tau(\theta)/\tau_s = \sigma_{eq}(\theta)/\sigma_{eq} \qquad (2)$$

where $\sigma_{eq}(\theta) = (\sigma_b(\theta)^2 + 3\tau(\theta)^2)^{1/2}$.

Yuhara and Tashimo(1987) showed the results of arranging the experimental data of NACA(Lundquist,1935), based on the equation given above.(See Fig.6) It is shown by Yuhara and Tashimo(1987) that the effects of plasticity can be evaluated by another equation given below,

$$1/(\sigma_p)^2 = 1/(\sigma_{eq})^2 + 1/(\sigma_y)^2 \qquad (3)$$

Buckling occurs, when $\sigma_{eq}(\theta)$ equals to σ_p.

AN EXPERIMENTAL STUDY ON SHEAR BUCKLING OF FAST BREEDER REACTOR MAIN VESSEL

Described as the example of experimental studies herein is the shear buckling test results shown in 1-7 of Table 1. Fig.7 shows a configuration of the fast breeder reactor structure. The main vessel of the structure is hanged from the roof slab at the upper end. In the vessel, there are internal structures, such as reactor core, etc., including the hot liquid sodium (maximum 510℃). Therefore, the reactor vessel has severe temperature gradient near the liquid sodium surface, while it has much lower internal pressure than that of light water reactor. Thus, the main vessel can be advantageously reduced the plate thickness considering the main vessel integrity against seismic loads. It requires sufficient plate thickness against buckling. The existing design codes, however, have not specified sufficiently the elastic-plastic shear buckling of such a relative short cylinder as the main vessel of fast breeder reactor. The studies, therefore, are required to be made, with consideration given to such conditions peculiar to the fast breeder reactor and to the seismic loads.

In this experiment, transverse shearing loads are applied via the screw jack under displacement control. The specimens were made of Type 304 stainless steel with diameter of 1 meter. Heater was located inside the specimen so that the experiment could be made at high temperature or under conditions of temperature distribution. A coil spring could be used to apply axial tensile stress, which acted on the main vessel due to the dead weight. Fig.8 shows an example of the load-displacement relation of the cylinder with temperature distribution as shown in Fig.9. From this, it can be seen that the load decreases considerably slowly even beyond the buckling load. Buckling stresses at uniform temperture can be estimated based on ϕ-method using theoretical elastic torsional buckling stress and shear yield stress as follows, (Galletly,Blachut,1985)

$$1/(\tau_{cr})^2 = 1/(\tau_s)^2 + 1/(\tau_y)^2 \qquad (4)$$

As a result, good estimation can be obtained. Even for cylinders with a temperature distribution, the estimation by the use of material properties determined at the higher temperature portion can also give good results.

The results described above are shown in Figs.10 and 11, together with the results of studeis already made by the use of metal specimens in other places. In Fig.10, the axis of abscissas takes R/t and the axis of ordinates takes the values of shear buckling stress normalized with elastic torsional buckling stress. In

1762

Fig.11, the axis of ordinates takes the buckling shear stress normalized with the simple evaluation value using ϕ-method. From Fig.10, it can be observed that R/t range of approximately 100 thru 300 is transient area. From Fig.11, it can be seen that the plasticity reduction was achieved considerably well by the ϕ-method.

CONCLUSION

Recent studies are introduced concerning the studies on the shear buckling of cylindrical shells in conjunction with the buckling of main vessels of fast breeder reactors due to seismic loads. Those recent experimental and analytical studies have been accumulating the data on buckling due to transverse shearing load such a short cylinder with R/t of about 200 and L/R of about unity, including the effect of high temperature (distribution).

These studies are now clarifying the effects of those parameters which govern buckling. In the near future, a reasonable design guide is urged to be established.

REFERENCES

The High Pressure Gas Safety Institute of Japan, Vibration Test Comittee (1982), (in Japanese), J. High Pressure Gas,Vol.19,No.10,497-518

The High Pressure Gas Safety Institute of Japan, Vibration Test Comittee (1982), (in Japanese), J. High Pressure Gas,Vol.21,No.7,363-373,No.8,440-452,No.9, 512-529

Akiyama,H. Yuhara,T. Shimizu,S. Takahashi,T. (1985),Limit State of Steel Cylindricl Structures under Earthquake Loadings, Proc. IUTAM SYMPOSIUM

Takayanagi,M. Kokubo,K. Nagashima,H. (1985),(in Japanese),Trans. Japan Soc. Mech. Engrs,Vol.51,No.462,539-544

Nagashima,H. Kokubo,K. Takayanagi,M. Saito,K. Imaoka,T. (1986), (in Japanese), Trans. Japan Soc. Mech. Engrs,Vol.52,No.479,1643-1648

Nagashima,H. Kokubo,K. Takayanagi,M. Saito,K. (1986),(in Japanese),Trans. Japan Soc. Mech. Eng.,Vol.52,No.479,1648-1654

Choi,H. Tanami,T. Hnagai,Y. (1986),(in Japanese),J. Structural and Construction Eng.(Trans. Architectual institute of Japan),No.369,60-68

Akiyama,H. Takahashi,M. Hashimoto,S. (1897),(in Japanese),J. Structural and Construction Eng.(Trans. Architectual institute of Japan),No.371,44-51

Kokubo,K. Shigeta,M. Madokoro,M. Sakurai,A. Nakamura,H. (1987), Trans. 9th Int. conference on SMiRT,Vol.E,167-172

Kawamoto,Y. Yuhara,T. Tashimo,M. Sakurai,A. Nakamura,H. (1987), Trans. 9th Int. conference on SMiRT,Vol.E,225-230

Nakamura,H. Matsuura,S. Sakurai,A. (1987), Trans. 9th Int. conference on SMiRT, Vol.E,219-224

Baker,W.E. Bennet,J.G. (1984), Nuclear Eng. Design,Vol.79,211-216

Butler,T.A. Baker,W.E. Bennet,J.G. Babcock,C.D. (1986), Nuclear Eng. Design,Vol.94, 31-39

Galletly,G.D. Blachut,J. (1985), J. Pressure Vessel Technology,Vol.107,101-106

Akiyama,H. Yuhara,T. (1985), Note on Buckling Problem in Earthquake-Resistant Limit-State Design

Yuhara,T. Tashimo,M (1987),Proceeding of Recent Experimental Research for Buckling Design Method of FBR Component,2nd International Seminar on Design Codes and Structural Mechanics

Lundquist,E.E. (1935),Strength tests of thin walled duralumin cylinders in combined transverse shear and bending,NACA-TN-No.523

TABLE. 1 Experimental study of buckling of cylindrical shell under transverse shearing loads (in Japan)

No.	Author(Organization)	Publication	Object	Feature
1-1	The High Pressure Gas Safety Institute of Japan, National Research Center for Disaster Prediction, MITI	1982	steel tower	R=600,R/t=260,400 5 real scale steel models
1-2	The High Pressure Gas Safety Institute of Japan, Nuclear Power Engineering Test Center, MITI	1984	steel tank	R=500,R/t=1562 1 mild steel model
1-3	Akiyama and colleagues,(Power Reactor and Nuclear Fuel Development Corp., Mitsubishi Heavy Industries)	1985	steel containment vessel	R=1300,R/t=650 9 shear } mild steel 6 compression } models
1-4	Takayanagi, Kokubo, Nagashima Nagashima and colleagues (Hitachi Ltd.)	1985 1986	tank	R=2500,R/t=625 1 Al model R=80,R/t=1600,816,332
1-5	Choi, Tanami, Hangai (Tokyo Univ.)	1986	cantileverd cylinder	R=150,R/t=150 4 Al, 6 steel models
1-6	Akiyama, Takahashi, Hashimoto (Tokyo Univ.)	1987	containment vessel,cylinder	R/t=104-1072 56 steel models
1-7	Kokubo and colleagues (CRIEPI, Hitachi Ltd.)	1987	FBR main vessel	R/t=750,300 polyester R/t=250,1250 6 Al R/t=200,286 20 stainless
	Kawamoto and colleagues (CRIEPI, Mitsubishi Heavy Industries)	1987	FBR main vessel	R=400,R/t=133,200,333 3 stainless steel models R/t=133 1 steel model
	Nakamura, Matsuura, Sakurai (CRIEPI)	1987	FBR main vessel	R=500,R/t=200 20 stainless steel models

unit (mm), R:radius, t:thickness, MITI : Ministry of International Trade and Industry
       CRIEPI : Central Research Institute of Electric Power Industry in Japan

TABLE. 2 Experimental study of buckling of cylindrical shell under transverse shearing loads
        (in foreign countries)

No.	Author(Organization)	Publication	Object	Feature
2-1	Butler, Baker, Bennet, Babcock (LANL,NRC)	1984 1986	steel containment vessel	R/t=458 Lexan models
2-2	Galletry, Blachut (Liverpool Univ.)	1985	FBR main vessl	R/t=125-188, R=150 14 steel models

Fig.1a Buckling Mode(Shear)

Fig.1b Buckling Mode(Axial Compression)

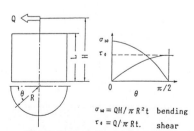

$\sigma_w = QH/\pi R^2 t$ bending
$\tau_\theta = Q/\pi R t.$ shear

Fig.2 Shearing and Bending
Stress Distribution

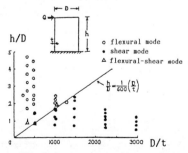

Fig.3 Mode of Buckling

1764

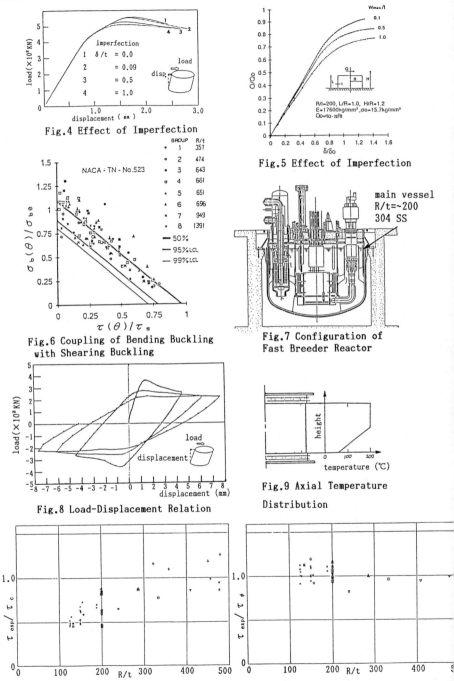

Fig.4 Effect of Imperfection

Fig.5 Effect of Imperfection

Fig.6 Coupling of Bending Buckling with Shearing Buckling

Fig.7 Configuration of Fast Breeder Reactor

Fig.8 Load-Displacement Relation

Fig.9 Axial Temperature Distribution

Fig.10 Buckling Stress Normalized with elastic Buckling Stress

Fig.11 Buckling Stress Normalized with φ-method Buckling Stress

EVALUATION OF BUCKLING AND COLLAPSE OF CYLINDRICAL VESSEL
DUE TO EARTHQUAKE LOADINGS

T. YUHARA

Mitsubishi Heavy Industries, Nagasaki R&D Center
Nagasaki, Japan

ABSTRACT

Buckling resistance under seismic motions is discussed for thin-walled
cylindrical vessels, of which predominant mode of failure is bending and
shear buckling under horizontal earthquake loadings.   Basic
characteristics of buckling and post buckling behaviors are investigated.
To evaluate the seismic resistance, dynamic loading effects on occurrence
of buckling and post buckling is important.   Ultimate limit state in the
post-buckling region is evaluated by the energy concept.

KEYWORDS

Buckling;post-buckling;cylindrical vessel;shear buckling;ultimate limit
design;seismic resistant design;earthquake loading.

INTRODUCTION

Accordingly to the need for the Fast Breeder Reactor (FBR) plants many
buckling research programs have been carried out in Japan and France.
Components of FBR are thin-walled shell structure under high temperature
and low pressure conditions.   The dominant design loads to the vessel and
piping are the seismic load and thermal loading, which play the important
roles in deciding the stiffeness of component and the types of their
support structure.   So far design method and evaluation for buckling and
collapse failure depend on the pressure vessel code.   The design
recommendation for primary stress limit (collapse) and buckling against
extreme loads are based on the plastic instability by internal pressure and
buckling due to external pressure and axial loads.   Recent design code
such as ETSTG(1980) and RCC-MR(1985) have tried to get out of pressure
vessel code toward the code for the thermal and earthquake loadings.   The
efforts have been continued for establishing the suitable design method and
evaluation method on the basis of the buckling and collapse behaviors
peculiar to the thin-walled shell structure under thermal and severe
earthquake loadings.

PRIMARY STRESS LIMITS AND BUCKLING CRITERIA IN PRESSURE VESSEL CODE

Table.1 shows the primary stress limit in the case of evaluation by elastic analysis. Primary stress limit for loading level C and D should be reexamined according to the collapse behavior of thin-walled vessels under strong earthquake loading. Especially to the plastic collapse behavior in the parts of the gross structural discontinuity of shell structure, such as knuckle and junction parts under mechanical loadings. Wada and Tashimo (1987) discussed such a problem.
Table.2 shows the buckling criteria and factor of safety in the pressure vessel code recommendation, which uses the imperfection factors (knock-down factors) and factor of safety respectively both to the types of shells and load patterns. Table.3 shows the lists of the factor of safety in existing code recommendations, which are not consistent among each other. The margin of safety against buckling due to strong earthquake loading should been studied in the case of thin-walled cylindrical structure under earthquake motions, which are dynamic in nature and repeated ones during very short time.

TABLE 1 Stress Limit by Elastic Analysis in Pressure
Vessel Design Code

Loading Code Ⴖ	Primary Stress Limit		Primary+Secondary Stress Limit
	P_m	P_L or P_L+P_b	$(P_L+P_b+Q)_R$
Design Level A & B	$S_m (0.9S_y)$	$1.5S_m (1.35S_y)$	$3S_m$
Level C	$1.2S_m (1.1S_y)$	$1.8S_m (1.6S_y)$	———
Level D	$\min \begin{cases} 2.4S_m (2.2S_y) \\ 0.7S_u \end{cases}$	$\min \begin{cases} 3.6S_m (3.2S_y) \\ 1.05S_u \end{cases}$	———

- S_m = Min.$[1/3S_u^{R.T.}, 2/3S_y^{R.T.}, 1/3S_u^T, 0.9S_y^T]$ for Austenite Strainless Steel. ( ) is when $S_m = 0.9S_y$.

TABLE 2 Factor of Safety in ASME PV & B Sec.III

Type	Load	Knock down factor	Factor of Safety		
			A & B	C	D
Cylinder	Axial Compression	0.207	2.0	1.67	1.34
Cylinder	External Pressure	1.00	3.0	2.5	2.0
Sphere	External Pressure	0.207	4.0	3.3	2.5

TABLE 3 Factor-of-Safety Against Load Controlled
         Buckling

Code Loading Level	Class 1		Class 2			
	ASME N-47	RCC-MR	ASME N-284		*3 MITI 501	
Design loading Level A & B	3.0	2.5	*1 2.4	*2 2.0	——	
Level C	2.5	2.0	2.0	1.67	*4 1.5 ~ 1.0	
Level D	1.5	1.3	1.6	1.34	*4 1.5 ~ 1.0	

* 1 Overall buckling   * 2 Local buckling

* 3 Seismic resistant design guideline

* 4 1.5 for elastic buckling , 1.0 for plastic collapse for S_1 and S_2
     earthquake loadibg, 1.0 to 1.5 for elasto - plastic buckling

BUCKLING AND POST-BUCKLING BEHAVIOR

For a self-standing, or suspended, thin-walled cylindrical vessels under
horizontal earthquakes, the primary loading conditions is declined bending
moment accompanied with transverse shear force.   In the case of the
thin-walled and short cylinder, the predominate mode of buckling is elastic
and elastic-plastic shear buckling coupled with bending one.
In existing design codes, such a buckling modes are evaluated by the
combination of tortional buckling with axial buckling.   Following the
recent numerous buckling tests of cylinder under transverse shear forces,
the evaluation method becomes possible to predict the interactive buckling
from pure bending and pure shear continuously in elastic-plastic buckling
due to combined bending and shear loading (Yuhara and Tashimo, 1987).
The example is shown in Fig.1 in the case of elastic buckling.
A number of buckling tests of thin-walled cylindrical structure under such
load conditions shows that they have the stable load displacement relation
adequated deformation capacity beyond the buckling.   Furthermore to
repeated transverse loadings, the stable load-displacement hysteresis were
obtained with regular characteristics (Akiyama, et al. 1985, 1986).   Fig.2
shows the such load-displacement relations in the case of (a) elastic and
(b) elastic-plastic shear buckling. Such a results of load-displacement
relationship shows that a simplified rules for hysteresis and restoring
force characteristics could be produced.
Furthermore it can be seen that energy absorption capacity of these
cylinders after buckling due to reciprocal transverse loads is tremendous
large compared with elastic or elastic-plastic strain energy before
buckling.   Such adequate deformation capacities and stable restoring force
characteristics are very important when the evaluation for seismic
resistance is investigated from standpoint of energy concept, in which the
energy input imported by earthquake to structures is compared with the
energy absorption capacity of the structures.

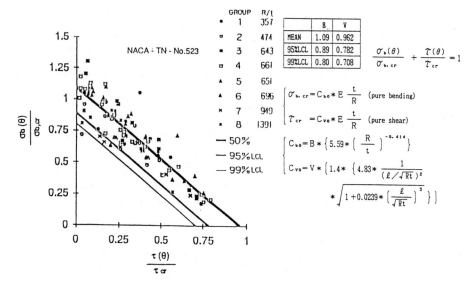

Fig. 1. Coupling of Bending Buckling with Shearing
Buckling.

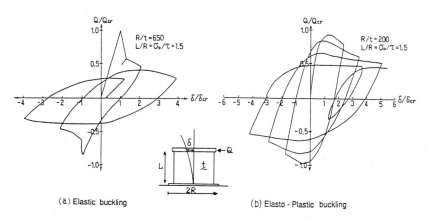

(a) Elastic buckling

(b) Elasto - Plastic buckling

Fig. 2. Load Displacement Relationship in Buckling and
Post-Buckling Behavior Due to Transverse Shear
Loading.

BEHAVIOR UNDER EARTHQUAKE LOADINGS

Structural response including buckling due to earthquakes could be
investigated by dynamic tests on the vibration tables and/or by the
simplified nonlinear dynamic analysis.   One application of the specific
problem is shown in the case of elastic-plastic shear buckling of short
cylinder.
Fig.3 shows the results of the dynamic test on the vibration table, carried
out by Yuhara and Tashimio (1987) in MHI recentry.   A model is an aluminum

cylinder with R/T (radius-to-thickness ratio) equal to 200 and L/R
(length-to-radius ratio) equal to 1.0.   The ratio of the maximum bending
stress to maximum shearing stress is equal to 1.5.   Load-displacement
relationships of this cylinder in the static buckling test are shown in
Fig.2(b), which has a typical elastic-plastic shear buckling mode.   The
Elcentro NS seismic waves was selected as input ground motions, of which
maximum acceleration α_{max} are scaled and changed stepwise upwards.   The
behaviors are divided to three parts, that is, linear elastic, nonlinear
response before buckling and post-buckling behavior to limit state.
Due to the elastic-plastic response before buckling, the maximum
acceleration of seismic waves which causes the buckling in the test is
higher than that which is estimated to cause buckling by linear elastic
response.
Occurrence of buckling did not mean the catastrophic failure or in mediate
collapse.   While the rate of the increase of the maximum displacement δ_{max}
keeps at a constant state by changing the stepwise the higher intensity of
maximum acceleration of the same waves, the rate of increase of δ_{max} become
rapidly and reach ultimate limit state.
Results of non-linear dynamic analysis of one-degree-of-freedom
system(SDOF) are shown in this figure, too.   Nonlinear spring constant of
which is the restoring force characteristics of regarding type, modelized
from experimental hysteresis loop shown in Fig.2(b).
The result shows that such analysis can simulate the fundamental property
of post buckling behavior under seismic motion.

ENERGY INPUT CONCEPT AND LIMIT STATE SEISMIC RESISTANT DESIGN

Akiyama, et al.(1985) discussed limit state of a more thin-walled
cylindrical vessel from standpoint of energy concept.
The load-displacement relationships under repeated transverse load are
obtained from buckling tests of large, fabricated steel cylinder model
under transverse loading, simulating overturning moment accompanied with
transverse shear force during the horizontal loadings.   Hysteresis loop
under repeated loading is shown in Fig.2(a).   Nonlinear dynamic
analysis(SDOF) system is carried out.   By changing the stepwise the
maximum acceleration of various seismic motion with no dumping system, the
limit state in post buckling regions was investigated to compare the
intensity of seismic motion with the energy input by earthquakes to buckled
structure (equal to energy absorption E_D in the case of no damping system)
and with the maximum displacement δ_{max}.
The ultimate limit where the energy absorption E_D and maximum displacement
commerce to show a rapid rate of increase is reached when the severity of
the earthquake γ reached to a certain as follow.

$$\gamma = \frac{\text{maximum acceleration } \alpha_{max} \text{ of input seismic waves}}{\text{maximum acceleration of input seismic waves equal to } \alpha_{cr}}$$

(which cause just the buckling displacement δ_{cr})

$$= 1.67$$

Energy absorption rate V_D/V_E increased with a constant rate when the
intensity of earthquake γ increased below the limit state.

$$\frac{V_D}{V_E} = \sqrt{\frac{E_D}{(1/2)Q_{cr}\delta_{cr}}} = \sqrt{\frac{W_p+W_e}{W_e}} = 1.5\gamma \qquad \text{when } \gamma < 1.67$$

Where W_e is elastic strain energy to buckling and W_p is energy absorption caused by the inelastic strain energy in post buckling deformation. E_D is energy input to structure, and V_D is equivalent velocity.

Such a plastification is a significant future of the high frequency structures while the energy input in the lower frequency structures such as buildings is generally stable amount, shown in Fig.4 by Yuhara(1987).

To more general modification from above mentioned research, Akiyama(1987) clarified the ultimate seismic resistance of buckled cylindrical structures.   The damage index was selected to be the maximum deflection while the loading index was selected to be the total input to a structure due to an earthquake.

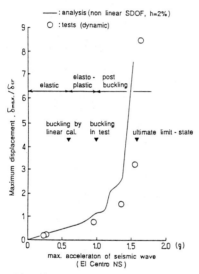

Fig. 3.   Elasto-Plastic Shear
Buckling under
Earthquake Loadings.

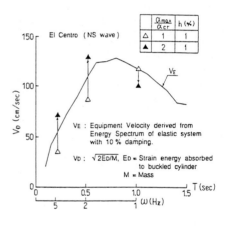

Fig. 4.   Energy input into Elastic
Buckling System (Dynamic
Analysis by S.D.O.F. for
Hysteresis in Fig.2(a)).

CONCLUSION

In order to evaluate the seismic resistance of a thin-walled cylindrical vessel, of which predominant mode of failure is buckling, it should be considered from the next three standpoints;

    (1)   to estimate the buckling and collapse strength peculiar to thin-walled vessels under predominant load patterns during earthquakes

    (2)   to understand the loading effects of earthquakes, which is dynamic in nature and repeated one during very short time.

    (3)   to take into account the limit state beyond the buckling and to investigate the margin from such a limit state on the basis of energy concept.

REFERENCES

Akiyama,H., Yuhara,T., Shimizu,S. and Takahashi,T.(1985). Limit state of
  steel cylindrical structure under earthquake loadings., _IUTAM symposium
  on lnelastic behavior of plates and shells_, Rio de Janeiro.
Akiyama,H., Takahashi,T. and Hashimoto,S.(1987). Buckling tests of steel
  cylindrical shell subjected to combined bending and shear, _Trans. of
  Architectural Institute of Japan, No.31_.
Akiyama,H.(1987). Post buckling behavior of steel cylindrical shells
  during earthquakes., _9th-SMiRT---K7/10_
ASME(1986). Boiler and Pressure Vessel Code Sec.III Nuclear component, NB,
  Code Case N-47, Chase 1 components in elevated temperature.
ASME(1980). Boiler and Pressure Vessel Code Case N-284, Metal containment
  shell buckling design method., Section III, Division 1, Class MC.
Baylac,G.(ed).(1984). Recent advance in nuclear component testing and
  theoretical studies on buckling, _ASME, PVP Conference_, San Antonio.
Choi,H.S., Tanami,T, and Hangai,Y.(1986). Failure tests of cantilevered
  cylindrical shells under a transverse load., _Pressure IASS Symposium_,
  Osaka, 1986, Vol.1, Elsevier Science Publishers B.V., Amsterdam.
Kawamoto,Y., Yuhara,T., Tashimo,M., Sakurai,A. and Nakamura,H.(1987).
  Plastic buckling of short cylinders under transverse shearing loads, _9th
  SMiRT_.
MITI(1980). Technical Standard for Structural Design, of facilities of
  nuclear power plant, MITI NOTICE, No.51, MITI, Regulatory guide for
  standard for design against earthquake of nuclear power plant.
Miller,C.D.(1984). Research related to buckling design of nuclear
  containment, _nuclear engineering and design, Vol.79, No.2_.
PNC(1980). Elevated temperature structural design guide for class 1
  components of prototype fast breeder reactor(ETSDG).
RCC-MR(1985). Design and manufacturing rules for fast reactors, AFCEN.
Yuhara,T. and Tashimo, M.(1987). Recent experimental research for buckling
  design method of FBR component., 2nd. International Seminar on "_Design
  Codes and Structural Mechanics_" Lausanne-Switzerland.
Wada,H. and Tashimo, M.(1987). Some notes on the structural design code
  for FBR components., ibid.

LIST OF ATTENDEES

Abe N .... Japan
Ahola E .... Finland
Akiyama H .... Japan
Ambrose S .... Australia
Arav F .... The Netherlands
Arnesson T .... Sweden
Au–Yang M K .... United States
Autrusson B .... France

Bai X S .... People's Republic of China
Bamford W H .... United States
Bao L .... People's Republic of China
Bao X F .... People's Republic of China
Bazergui A .... Canada
Bernstein M D .... United States
Blach A E .... Canada
Brocks W .... Federal Republic of Germany
Brunovsky M .... Czechoslovakia
Bush S H .... United States

Cai H Q .... People's Republic of China
Cai Z P .... People's Republic of China
Capitanescu T D .... Canada
Cesari F G .... Italy
Chen C K .... People's Republic of China
Chen C Q .... People's Republic of China
Chen D F .... People's Republic of China
Chen G L .... People's Republic of China
Chen J J .... People's Republic of China
Chen S N .... People's Republic of China
Chen W Q .... People's Republic of China
Chen Y Y .... People's Republic of China
Cheng S Z .... People's Republic of China
Combescure A .... France
Corbett C B .... United Kingdom
Cuan F Q .... People's Republic of China

Dahlberg L .... Sweden
Dai S H .... People's Republic of China
Daman E L .... United States
Deng J D .... People's Republic of China
Deuster G .... Federal Republic of Germany
Dietrich D E .... United States

Edelmann X .... Switzerland
Erve M .... Federal Republic of Germany

Farr J R .... United States
Feng D Z .... People's Republic of China

Feng X Z .... People's Republic of China
Fettahlioglu O A .... United States
Fischer K ...... Federal Republic of Germany
Flaman M T .... Canada
Flesch B .... France
Fong J T .... United States
Francesco C .... Italy
Fukuyama S .... Japan
Furusawa J .... Japan

Gao C J .... People's Republic of China
Gasiak G .... Poland
Gayk W .... Federal Republic of Germany
Ge S X .... People's Republic of China
Gerardo D A .... Italy
Gerlach H D .... Federal Republic of Germany
Gowda B C .... United States
Grandemange J M .... France
Groome R D .... United Kingdom
Gu Z M .... People's Republic of China
Gümpel P .... Federal Republic of Germany
Guo D F .... People's Republic of China
Guo L .... People's Republic of China

Hao S .... People's Republic of China
Hessling G .... Sweden
Higuchi M .... Japan
Hoffmann W ..... Federal Republic of Germany
Hojo K .... Japan
Hollinger G L .... United States
Holt A E .... United States
Hong D X .... People's Republic of China
Hong Y J .... People's Republic of China
Hotka P .... Federal Republic of Germany
Hou Y X .... People's Republic of China
Hsu K H .... United States
Hu B H .... People's Republic of China
Huang N Z .... People's Republic of China
Huang W X .... People's Republic of China
Huang Z Z .... People's Republic of China
Huo L X .... People's Republic of China
Hyde T H .... United Kingdom

Ibels H .... Federal Republic of Germany
Igari T .... Japan
Iida K .... Japan
Imai M .... Japan
Ingham T .... United Kingdom

Salcher A .... Austria
Samuelson L A .... Sweden
Sandstrom R .... Sweden
Sang Z F .... People's Republic of China
Sawa T .... Japan
Schneider R O ... Federal Republic of Germany
Shao Z G .... People's Republic of China
Shaw J B .... United Kingdom
Shen S M .... People's Republic of China
Shimomura J .... Japan
Shou P N .... People's Republic of China
Solomos G .... Italy
Song G Y .... People's Republic of China
Song H M .... People's Republic of China
Song M C .... People's Republic of China
Spenidel M O .... Switzerland
Stanley P .... United Kingdom
Stark J M .... New Zealand
Sturm D .... Federal Republic of Germany
Su D Z .... People's Republic of China
Sui M Z .... People's Republic of China
Sugino M .... Japan
Sun G F .... People's Republic of China
Sun G L .... People's Republic of China
Sun G Y .... People's Republic of China
Sun T C .... People's Republic of China
Swanson J A .... United States

Tahara T .... Japan
Takaiwa K .... Japan
Takemata H .... Japan
Tanaka Y .... Japan
Tang Y G .... People's Republic of China
Tang Z A .... People's Republic of China
Tanimura M .... Japan
Tao X .... People's Republic of China
Timashev S A .... The Soviet Union
Tomimatsu M .... Japan
Tong W W .... People's Republic of China
Tsuchida Y .... Japan
Tsukimori K .... Japan

Udoguchi T .... Japan
Umemoto T .... Japan

Vaccari V .... Italy
Valtonen O .... Finland
Vignes A .... France

Wang G M .... People's Republic of China
Wang H Z .... People's Republic of China

Wang J H .... People's Republic of China
Wang K F .... People's Republic of China
Wang L B .... People's Republic of China
Wang M O .... People's Republic of China
Wang R G .... People's Republic of China
Wang S Q .... People's Republic of China
Wang X C .... People's Republic of China
Wang X S .... People's Republic of China
Wang Y C .... People's Republic of China
Wang Y D .... People's Republic of China
Wang Y P .... People's Republic of China
Wang Y X .... People's Republic of China
Wang Z C .... People's Republic of China
Wang Z H .... People's Republic of China
Wang Z Q .... People's Republic of China
Wang Z R .... People's Republic of China
Wang Z X .... People's Republic of China
Wang Z Y .... People's Republic of China
Watanabe O .... Japan
Wei L F .... People's Republic of China
Werber K .... Federal Republic of Germany
Widera G E O .... United States
Wong Y C .... United Kingdom
Wu D G .... People's Republic of China
Wu F W .... People's Republic of China
Wu G S .... People's Republic of China
Wu J S............ People's Republic of China
Wu Y .... People's Republic of China
Wu Z J .... People's Republic of China
Wu Z Q .... People's Republic of China

Xia R L .... People's Republic of China
Xiao J S .... People's Republic of China
Xiao Y G.......... People's Republic of China
Xie K G........... People's Republic of China
Xu H .... People's Republic of China
Xu X F .... People's Republic of China
Xue D D .... People's Republic of China
Xue J L .... People's Republic of China
Xue K S .... People's Republic of China
Xue M D .... People's Republic of China

Yamamoto Y .... Japan
Yamauchi K .... Japan
Yang F Y .... People's Republic of China
Yang Z D .... People's Republic of China
Yang Z G.......... People's Republic of China
Yin H Z........... People's Republic of China
Yu T H .... People's Republic of China
Yu X H .... People's Republic of China
Yu Z K .... People's Republic of China

ERRATA

to

Sixth International Conference on Pressure Vessel Technology
Volume 1: Design & Analysis

"Why Layered Wall Inner Shells Do Not Buckle" by R T Tschiersch, W Huessler, and K Werber

page 330 in caption of Fig.6, "b=3.2mm" should read "b=4.5mm"

page 333 Delete Fig.10,and substitute **page 334** Delete Fig.11,and substitute the following:

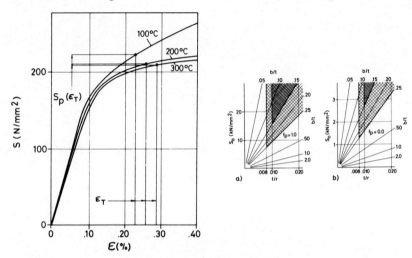

page 335 Delete Fig.13, and substitute the following:

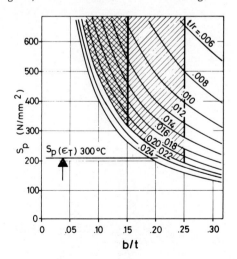

"On the Design of the ¢800 Wire-wound Superhigh Pressure Vessel"
by Dazeng Su

page 341   In the sixth line, "by winding the winding the wire" should read
"by winding the wire"

Volume 2: Materials & Fabrication

"Plant Construction Cost Simulation Based on Energy required and Its Cost"
by K Takaiwa

page 1274   in Eq.(10),   "$\xi_m = \dfrac{\Sigma mh}{\Sigma Mh}$" should read   "$\xi_m = \dfrac{\Sigma mh}{\Sigma Mh} - 1$"

in Eq.(12),   "$\pi = \dfrac{\Sigma MH / \Sigma Mh}{\xi_m + \xi_a}$" should read   "$\pi = \dfrac{\Sigma MH / \Sigma Mh}{1 + \xi_m + \xi_a}$"

in Eq.(13),   "$= \dfrac{\xi_m \beta_m + \xi_a \beta_a}{\xi_m + \xi_a}$" should read   "$= \dfrac{1 + \xi_m \beta_m + \xi_a \beta_a}{1 + \xi_m + \xi_a}$"

in the Sixth line from the bottom, "as follows" should read "where
mh = Mh, as follows:"